VOYAGES OF A SIMPLE SAILOR

ROGER D. TAYLOR

VOYAGES OF A SIMPLE SAILOR

𝓕

THE FITZROY PRESS

Published by The FitzRoy Press 2008

$\mathcal{F}$

The FitzRoy Press
5 Regent Gate
Waltham Cross
Herts EN8 7AF

ISBN 978-0-9558035-0-5

A catalogue record for this book is available from the British Library

Publishing management by Troubador Publishing Ltd, Leicester, UK
Printed in the UK by The Cromwell Press Ltd, Trowbridge, Wilts.

*This book is dedicated to my father, Angus Taylor,
who at eighty-seven years of age can still keep us
enthralled with his own tales of the sea.*

In order to minimise the cost and ecological impact of this book, colour photographs have been omitted. Galleries of photographs linked to this text can be found at www.thesimplesailor.com

Contents

Preface

'No, when I go to sea, I go as a simple sailor...'
Herman Melville, *Moby Dick*

The first two of these three voyages took place many years ago. In the intervening decades people would often suggest I write about them. The time never seemed right. I never felt ready. I thought I would probably never do it. But, in the strange way that life's patterns assert themselves, the time suddenly arrived when I not only felt ready to revisit and write down these experiences, I felt thoroughly compelled to do so. All of a rush I wanted to get it all down on paper. Maybe the years of quiet distillation in some deep inner vault had brought the memories and images to their proper maturity. Maybe they had been waiting for the right moment to assert themselves, to be decanted from those barrels lying long immobile and untapped in some dark corner of my mind, to be brought up, poured into a clear fresh glass and held up for examination against the piercing, uncomfortable daylight of this new century.

All action needs a catalyst, and there is no doubt that it was my most recent voyage in *Mingming* that acted as such. The preparation and conduct of that little adventure, the third described in this book, flowed directly from the ocean experiences of over thirty years ago. I scarcely realised it at the time. The rush and excitement of finding and rebuilding a suitable small yacht, and sailing her, engine-less, down to Plymouth, all while I was running my business, precluded much considered thinking about how the present linked with the past. It was only later that I started to reflect on the logical threads that ran through all three voyages, how they all made sense of each other. Having seen the sense of it all, I realised that I could, at last, write about it...

PART ONE

SHIPWRECK

I have scarcely found a semblance of sleep in the heaving forepeak when a scream, terrifying for its naked conviction, comes down the hatch – All hands on deck and bring your lifejackets! The words force themselves through my shell of semi-consciousness. They reverberate in my unwilling head, which knows already what they mean but that, for just one heartbeat, attempts to ignore them, to forget them, to pretend they never existed. Not possible. It is not possible to ignore them. Nor is it possible to ignore their meaning, nor their implication. There is no escaping them. At the second heartbeat I am fully awake and my stomach lurches. This, I know, is finally it. For three days, since weathering the North Cape of New Zealand, we have been fighting for survival. Storm force winds from the north-east, the leftovers of a tropical storm that has wound its way down from the Pacific Islands, have swept in and pinned us between North Cape to the north, and Cape Karikari to the south. We are in the classic shipwreck position of the square-rigger – embayed between two headlands with an onshore gale and no way to sail out. Unless conditions change, there is only one outcome – the ship will be driven onto the hostile shore to leeward. The land is now close to, somewhere ahead in the blackness under our lee bow. We cannot tack ship in these conditions. To wear round on to a southerly tack would lose us another mile or so; bring us a mile closer to our certain demise. By midnight, an hour ago, when my watch turned in, grateful for some respite from the searing wind and rain, we knew there was little hope. Nothing overt was said, but the ship's complement was tense and sombre. Each man, and the one woman, had retreated to his or her own private contemplation of what now seemed inevitable. Little was said apart from the barest necessities for running the ship. The usual banter and backchat had evaporated. We were grim, deadly so. A simple and unvoiced question preoccupied every one of us – will I be alive by dawn? Or will I be dead? And if I am dead, what will be the manner of my dying?

1

I was living and working in Cairns, North Queensland, when I first read about the *Endeavour II*. By then I was twenty-three years old and was fully embarked on a life of adventure. At age eight I had run away from home to seek my fortune. An empty stomach brought me home by teatime. At ten I first went to sea, in a ten-foot dinghy. The owner and skipper was my best friend David. We sailed out into the tidal waters of the Dee estuary. This was strictly forbidden. We were supposed to be sailing within the confines of the marine lake. For the first time I saw a clear horizon from the deck of a small yacht – Liverpool Bay, where the great ships come and go to places beyond imagination. An inexpressible yearning was born, a need, a compulsion which haunts me to this day.

At age fifteen, by which time my long-suffering parents had accepted that their injunctions held little sway, I had hitchhiked around Western Europe. A head-on collision in the south of France had left me hospitalised in Nice for a week. Battered but undaunted, I carried on through northern Italy and Switzerland. The red mercurochrome that had been used to treat the lacerations on my face worked wonders in stopping sympathetic drivers. At seventeen, prior to going to university, I hitchhiked across Europe and Turkey to Iran, Iraq and Syria. This was a thirteen thousand mile round trip.

I took £40 with me and came home with £4 in my pocket. A little money was made on the way selling my blood in Greece and street busking in Istanbul.

After graduating I set off again, this time with a girl-friend. We hitchhiked across Europe, Turkey and Iran and on to Afghanistan, over the Khyber Pass to Pakistan and then by special train (there was a war on at the time) to India. We took respite from the teeming streets of Old Delhi with a trip up to the old colonial hill station of Mussoorie, in the Himalayan foothills.

Next stop was Bangkok, and escape from that noisy city to the calm and charm of Pattaya Beach on the Gulf of Siam. Pattaya is now a notorious destination for so-called sex tourists, a metropolitan nightmare of bars, hotels and broth-els selling every kind of sleaze to every kind of sleaze-bag. In the late sixties it was close to idyllic – a long curve of empty white sand, on the one side a clear turquoise sea, on the other groves of palms and bamboo hiding teak-built Thai houses on stilts. The idyll was offset, however, by the US Army Rest and Recreation Centre at the north end of the beach. The Vietnam war was in full swing. GI's were sent here on battle leave. We got to know some of the US soldiers and had access to some of their facilities – in particular their fleet of sailing dinghies.

On we went to Singapore, where my long hair marked me out as an undesirable. Our passports were confiscated and we were given just a few days to appear at one of their offices with a paid ticket out of the island state, when our passports would be returned to us. This put paid to the idea of trying to find passage on a merchant ship to the Philippines. The last of our money bought a flight to Perth, Western Australia.

Perth was booming. The already buoyant Western Australian mining industry had been given another boost by the discovery of uranium in the north-west. Downtown Perth was a mass of new high-rise office blocks under construction. I got a job as a carpenter's labourer, then graduated to carpenter and soon leading-hand carpenter. The money was good and we bought a keelboat – a twenty-one foot half-decker called *Sirius*. For a season we raced every weekend on the Swan River.

After fifteen months or so I left Perth on my own and travelled by train and ship to Tasmania. I fancied a change from dirty manual work, so applied for a job as a clerk in the Police Department. Instead, my interviewers, who evidently held some wider civil service brief, decided that I would be better employed as a schoolteacher. I was sent out to New Norfolk High School, about twenty-five miles up the Derwent River from Hobart, and was given two weeks' teacher training. This consisted of sitting in the back of various classrooms watching how it was done, after which I was given a full timetable teaching English and Social Studies. I was well-versed in English, but the latter was mainly Australian history, about which I knew absolutely nothing. Fortunately my pupils, in the main a bunch of little terrors from the darker Tasmanian hinterland, knew even less. I loved and often visited the western coast of Tasmania. Here, impenetrable rainforest and towering peaks spill down to windswept beaches where the surf, meeting land for the first time thousands of miles from the coasts of South America, and driven on by the relentless westerlies of the Roaring Forties, starts breaking and pounding a good mile out to sea.

I taught for six months, keeping a page or two ahead of my students in the history textbook. Then I took the car ferry to Melbourne, and traded in my Mini for a Holden panel van – an Aussie workhorse conceived for the bush. The bush was where I was heading. For four months I wound my way through the outback of Australia. I drove seventy or eighty miles a day, usually on roads of red 'bull-dust', then pulled off into the bush. Mostly I slept under the stars, occasionally in the back of the van. For the first time, in the limpid southern air, I really saw the night sky. The hundred billion stars of our own galaxy pierced the black fastnesses of space in a wheeling light-show that literally made me dizzy in the contemplation of its scale. It was altogether a contemplative period. I walked mile after mile through the arid bush, disturbed only by the occasional hiss of a frilled lizard, or the distant thump of a marsupial under way. I had no company and was none the worse for that.

In central Queensland I walked on parched earth that had not known rain for fifteen years. It was layered like large dried soapflakes and my legs sank up to my calves at every step. Further on heavy rain did arrive, turning the bull-dust to a deep, terracotta porridge. My van slid off the road, up to its axles in mud, inextricable. I waited over a day before the next vehicle arrived, a big four by four truck, the cab crammed with young stockmen, the tray of the truck with their saddles. They hoiked me gaily out of the mire with much revving and muddy spinning of wheels, then sped off.

My walkabout ended in Cairns. I was running low on money and needed a job. There was not much on offer in the local paper, but Hayles Cruises, the company which more or less had the monopoly on tourist ferries for the northern part of the Barrier Reef, were advertising for a deckhand. I was interviewed by a humourless middle-aged chap, who I later learned was the boss's son-in-law, and heir-apparent to the Hayles' shipping dynasty. I got the job and started the next day. For two or three days each week I relieved on the Green Island run. Green Island is a coral island an hour or so out from Cairns. The boat was usually pretty full. Apart from the usual handling of lines, I helped serve tea and food from the ship's food hatch. At Green Island I skippered a glass-bottomed runabout, with about a dozen tourists aboard, over the reef.

However, my main job was as deckhand on the boat that went up to Cooktown and back once a week. Deckhand duties meant anything not done by the other two crewmembers – the skipper, who hated all passengers and never left the bridge, and the engineer, who hated all passengers and never left the engine room. On Mondays the ship's small hold was loaded with supplies, principally beer, for Cooktown, in those days almost inaccessible by road. I sweated down in the hold stacking crates and boxes while a small dockside crane, driven by the engineer, lowered them down. On Tuesdays we took on board thirty to forty passengers for the daylong trip to Cooktown. I had to cook and serve them lunch, then clear the tables and wash up. Lunch never once varied during the months I did it – boiled beef, boiled peas and boiled potatoes. Late on Tuesday afternoon we arrived at the rickety wharf at Cooktown, only a few yards from the beach where the great man had careened the real *Endeavour*, to repair her after her holing on the reef. Cooktown lies in about fifteen degrees south, so is unequivocally tropical. There was then just one dusty high street, with a general store, a couple of banks, and a profusion of pubs. The backdrop in every direction except the channel out to sea was of rain-forested hills. Nothing and nobody moved with any great speed. Old codgers, who lived in makeshift huts on the beach, fished off the wharf and yarned till midnight. It was a sleepy, somewhat sad backwater, a washed-up, end-of-the-line setting for a Conrad novel.

On Wednesday mornings we unloaded the hold, then took on the local produce for transport to Cairns. This was always lumps of locally mined tin, wrapped in sackcloth, and sacks and sacks of pineapples. Tin and pineapples. Once the loading was finished we had the rest of the day off, which usually meant fishing off the wharf and yarning with the old codgers. On Thursday we took on passengers for the return run down to Cairns. En route they were treated to boiled beef, boiled peas and boiled potatoes.

I never tired of the weekly voyage up the coast and back. An iridescent blue sea, a jungle-covered coastline with its twists and turns, further back all manner of strange mountainous topography – there was always something to look at and admire. Cook himself was always there for his naming of the coastline. At Cape Tribulation, so christened as his fate hung in the balance, a small boat always came off to collect the weekly mail and supplies from us.

In Cairns I rented a room on the ground floor of a little wooden house out in the suburbs. The owner, Anna Mignone, a genteel Queensland grandmother of Italian descent, lived, as did most north Queenslanders, on the first floor. The garden had a huge mango tree, laden with fruit and fruit bats. The house next door, a similar suburban wooden house over a low wooden fence, was the Cairns' brothel. Activities there were so discreet, and I was then so naïve, that I only discovered this when Anna one day announced it quite matter-of-factly. The frequent taxi arrivals and departures were then explained. A police patrol car came occasionally, and the officers would sit up in the first floor kitchen, on our side of the house and therefore visible, with the madame. I chatted with her a few times over the fence. I scarcely saw the girls. Apparently they came up from Brisbane and were changed frequently. One evening walking home late I saw a touching scene, through the wooden slats of a ground-floor bedroom – two girls in peignoirs on the bed, one sitting quietly while the other tenderly brushed and brushed her long hair for her.

As I sat out on my little veranda one evening, idly reading the local paper, an article jolted me out of my end-of-day torpor. There was a wooden square-rigged sailing ship, the *Endeavour II*, in Brisbane. She had previously been in Sydney as part of the Cook bicentennial celebrations. She had then sailed up to Brisbane and would soon be leaving for New Zealand and the Pacific Islands. Square-rigger...Pacific Islands...my imagination was already running riot... For years I had been reading the literature – Dana, Bullen, Villiers, Anson. A secret dream of sailing on a proper square-rigger had always seemed just that – an unattainable dream. There were now very few sailing ships. Most were modernised steel-hulled training ships, owned by various navies. Here was a privately-owned wooden ship, preparing for a long voyage. Sailing ships need big crews. I was young, healthy, footloose, and, having been both a sea scout and a naval cadet, at least knew the basics of sailing and seamanship. Maybe I could get a berth aboard her...

My excitement was growing. My head reeled with images of blue lagoons and swaying palms. I could feel the warm trade winds caressing my cheek and hear the distant breaking of surf on coral. Bare-breasted maidens, their voices chorusing seductive harmonies, hung garlands of headily-scented frangipani around my proffered neck. Hell, there was no time to lose! Within an hour I'd written and posted a letter to the ship, care of Patrick's Wharf, Brisbane, outlining my background and offering myself as crew. Within a week I had a letter back. They wanted me. Within two weeks I had handed in my notice and was on my way to Brisbane. At last I was to become a proper sailor and really taste the dangerous magic of the far horizon!

2

The *Endeavour II* had not always been thus named. She had started life just a few years earlier as the *Monte Cristo*. Built in Vancouver BC by a consortium of businessmen keen to recreate the great days of sail, she was, in overall dimensions, not dissimilar to Cook's *Endeavour*, but was altogether a sleeker, faster ship. She was built, along the lines of the brigantine *Albatross*, as published in Uffa Fox's *Second Book of Boats*. This was a fine choice indeed, and bold too; it is thought that the *Albatross* had never in fact been built.

Her incarnation, the *Endeavour II*, was, on the face of it, well built from the best materials, principally mahogany planking on heavy fir frames. Sitka spruce, light but strong, had been hewn from the nearby forests and fashioned into her mighty spars. The three-sectioned mainmast, tapering from its tree-like base to a section just a few inches in diameter at the truck, rose a majestic eighty-four feet off the deck. Her deck measured ninety-four feet but, with her long bowsprit and jibboom ranging forward, she stretched out to nearly a hundred and forty feet overall.

She was rigged as a three-masted barque, with square sails on the mainmast and foremast, and a gaff-rigged fore-and-aft spanker on the mizzenmast. With her four jibs set forward, and a variety of staysails, the *Endeavour II* could fly up to seventeen sails in all, a great billowing press of canvas, nine thousand square feet of it. This hefty rig, of baroque complexity, was held aloft and manipulated by five miles or so of running and standing rigging, all of natural hemp, manila, and galvanised wire. There were no mechanical winches on board – all pully-hauly was by block and tackle and brute strength. Small twin diesels, mainly for getting in and out of port and charging the ship's batteries, were the only engines aboard. Apart from a VHF radio, she had no electronic aids to navigation. There were few concessions to modernity. Creature comforts were few. She was, for the late twentieth century, as near as you could hope to get to the real thing.

After the usual disagreements and fall-outs that blight most well-meaning joint efforts, ownership of the newly-built vessel fell into the hands of the Canadian businessman Ron Craig. Ron had pale features topped off with a mop of shiny black curls – the perfect looks for his moneymaking scheme. For its first year or two the ship, as the *Monte Cristo*, worked its way down the western seaboard of the US. In port the crew dressed as eighteenth century sailors, with Ron himself decked out as the Count, and charged sightseers for a guided tour. Apparently the fast-talking and charismatic Ron had a great talent for luring the public on board. Just as well – the berthage and maintenance costs for such a vessel would be astronomic. Just what mishmash was fed to these Bermuda-shorted punters is hard to imagine, but who cared? It was marginally more real than Popeye, and it paid the bills. Ron was first and last an entrepreneur. He had little interest in the ship as a sailing vessel, and rarely sailed aboard her.

I don't know exactly when or how the idea took root, but at some point the connection was made between the dimensions and rig of the ship, and the imminent bicentenary of Cook's voyage to Australia and New Zealand. While not an *Endeavour* look-alike to the connoisseur, she was close enough for the man in the street and, more importantly, probably the only sailing ship in commission globally that looked so similar to the *Endeavour*. Despite the demeaning use to which she had been put, there was nevertheless a high degree of historical accuracy in her build and rig.

A plan of action was hatched. First her name would be changed to *Endeavour II*. She would then be sailed across the Pacific to Sydney, where she would be the centrepiece of the bicentennial celebrations of Cook's discovery of Botany Bay in 1770. This would be followed by a cruise up the Australian eastern seaboard, taking on paying sightseers at each port, in her new guise as Cook's flagship. She would then sail to New Zealand. There she would feature in further, belated, Auckland celebrations of Cook's arrival there in 1769, after which she would re-enact Cook's figure-of-eight voyage charting the coasts of the North and South Islands of New Zealand. After that – who knows? In fact, by the time I joined her, Ron had contracted for her to do charter work in the Fijian islands.

I knew nothing of all this as I arrived at the Brisbane dockside and surveyed my new home. She was magnificent indeed. Three masts, their yards neatly squared, towered above. The main yard was a prodigious timber spar, its ends projecting well beyond the deep bulwarks amidships. That was while the ship was upright. I could already see myself out on the leeward end of that spar with the ship well heeled in a big sea... Forward, the bowsprit and jibboom angled gently upwards for over forty feet. Now I was clinging to the outer end, gasketing a headsail as the bowsprit reared first skywards then plunged down into the face of the next wave. I shuddered with fearful delight.

Aft was a small poop deck with a low deck cabin – the

skipper's quarters and chart room. Amidships in the waist stood another deckhouse – the galley. A third deckhouse – the owner's quarters when he was on board, lay further forward. The teak deck planking ran straight fore and aft, broken only by the steps up to the poop deck aft and the raised fore-deck. The hull, sweetly-shaped and purposeful, was of varnished mahogany, the long seams leading the eye forward to a bearded, wild-eyed figurehead – the Count himself.

The summer air was heavy with the odours that emanated out from the hull and rig – an intoxicating mix of Stockholm tar, old rope, new rope, paint, varnish, tallow, timber, well-used canvas, all under-pinned by the harbourside taint of the river waters as they swirled their way seawards. It was the raw dockside smell of another age. I breathed it in deeply and hungrily. Was there anything that could evoke so completely the imminence of a sea-going adventure, and reinforce the timeless pull of the horizon?

What struck me most of all as I stood on the old timber quayside, overpowered by so many first impressions, was the sheer quantity of rope. Miles and miles of running rigging led to rows of belaying pins the length of the bulwarks, every one holding a great coil of thick hemp rope. Each mast base too had pin rails on three sides hung with yet more coils. Aloft was a dizzying maze of stays and rigging crisscrossing in every direction. I'd seen this sort of thing before – as a naval cadet I'd toured the *Victory* in Portsmouth. The *Endeavour II* was a minnow by comparison. But the *Victory* was essentially a museum piece – a dead ship. This was a real, live, floating square-rigger, soon to put to sea. What's more, I would be aboard her. I could scarcely believe my good luck.

3

I was welcomed aboard with a steely handshake and even steelier searching stare from the mate, Chris Scott, a squat, square, no-nonsense Australian. His natural aura of menace was enhanced by his thick but neatly-trimmed black beard.

Well, I thought, *here's your bucko mate if ever there was.* For his part his ebony, unflinching pupils continued to bore into me, searching, I knew, for some sign of weakness. *So what have we got here*, I could feel him thinking, *some bloody wingeing pom who fancies himself a sailor. We'll soon see about that.* I held his stare as best I could. *Sling your kit in the forepeak*, he said finally. *Find yourself an empty bunk, then get yourself back here. Got a job for you.*

I lugged my cardboard suitcase forward, and found my way down the hatch into the forepeak. In the gloom I could make out two rows of tiered bunks down each side, twelve in all. *G'day*, said a soft voice, startling me. One of the bunks was occupied. In the dim light I could make out the boyish face, under a thatch of unkempt reddish-blond hair, of a young guy stretched out on a lower berth, hands behind head. *I'm Pete*, said the boyish face. *Came aboard at Sydney an' still here. You the new guy? Roger*, I said. *Just got down here from Cairns. What bunk should I take? That one's free*, he said, pointing to an upper one on the port side. I hoisted my suitcase up and stowed it at the foot of the coffin-like space. *Well,* I said, *I'd better get back. Seems the mate's got a job for me. Aw yeah?* drawled Pete, with a sleepy grin, *might come on deck meself then.*

I came back up on deck into the humid air. Dark clouds were bubbling up overhead. The water of the Brisbane River swept past, grey and impersonal. A traitorous doubt crept into a corner of my mind. I had thrown in a great job, sold my car, staked everything on joining this ship – a ship about which I knew nothing. I'd been impelled by a fine romantic dream, but this was the reality. What if I don't get on with my shipmates? What if I don't measure up as a seaman? What if I simply don't like it? I stifled these thoughts with a grimace and made my way aft.

The mate was in the waist of the ship at the foot of the mainmast. He was chatting with an athletic-looking guy with curly blond hair and a deep-tanned complexion. He radiated good health and good humour. *This is Springer,* said the mate. *John Springer. The bosun. Hi Roger!* said Springer, grasping my hand. *Welcome aboard, man! Hear you bin workin' the boats up north.* I nodded. *Hell, that's great! Can always use someone with, you know, some experience? I bin with the ship since California. Signed on in San Diego? Love this ship, man! You wanna know anything, you juss ask, OK?* He gave me a final grin with a perfect set of dazzling teeth, then turned and padded off, panther-like, along the deck. It took a second or two for his energy to follow off behind him, leaving me to the silent mercy of the mate.

Right then, he said. *Like I said, got a little job for you.* For a few seconds he stroked his beard with a brawny palm, then suddenly pointed aloft. *See that top yard?* I nodded. *What's it called?* I hesitated. It was the fourth yard up. If the ship had single topsails, it would be the royal yard. If the ship had upper and lower topsails, it would be a topgallant yard. However, this wasn't a full-rigged ship, so it was unlikely the topsails would be split. I took the plunge – *Royal yard?* I stared at his face. His eyes softened, almost imperceptibly. *Course bloody not!* he suddenly shot back. *It's the main royal yard. Don't forget to always name the bloody mast, yer drongo!* I winced at the insult.

Now, he said, *see right out at the starboard end of the yard? Yeah? There's a rope coming off aft from it. See it?* Again I nodded. *Know what it is?* By now I had the idea – *Main royal yard starboard brace? That's better,* he said, his voice softening a bit. *Now,* he said, hardening up again, *you may not be able to see it from here, but the brace is shackled to the fitting at the end of the yard. Know what I mean?*

I stared upwards. Although the ship was immobile, the masts and yards seemed to be gyrating against the sky. For the first time I was properly aware of the mass and height of the rig. I focussed as best I could on the end of the royal yard – the main royal yard, about eighty feet above us. It was impossible to make out the detail of the brace-to-yard connection.

Well, I said, *I can't really see it from here, but I understand what you mean.* The mate pulled out a spanner attached to a lanyard. *Good,* he said. *Now, tie this spanner to your belt.* I took it from him, and started threading the lanyard around my belt. *Look around the deck,* he said. I did. *There's lots of people, aren't there?* He was right. Somehow the previously empty ship had become alive, with six or seven bronzed crewmen scattered the length of the deck, eyeing us with an air of amused expectancy.

Never, ever, ever, go aloft without your tools tied to you, continued the mate. *Even a small spanner dropped from fifty or sixty feet could kill someone on deck. Understand?* I nodded. My mouth was suddenly dry and I was sure I would just croak if I tried to talk. *Right,* he said, *that shackle we were talking about. Think it might be a bit loose. Nip up and tighten it for me would yer?*

4

Grasping the outer of the main shrouds, I swung myself up on top of the bulwark and got myself on to the first of the ratlines, the ropes seized horizontally across the main shrouds to make a ladder for climbing aloft. I looked aloft along the shrouds. There were four or five shrouds leading to the top of the first segment of the mast – the mainmast proper. At deck level these gave a comforting width to the ratlines – a good four feet. This narrowed as the shrouds converged on the maintop – the first set of crosstrees of the ascent. Before the crosstrees another set of shrouds, this time for the next section of the mast – the main topmast, came out from the mainmast and round the outside of the crosstrees. These were the futtock shrouds. To negotiate them properly meant hanging from them, climbing out away from the mast, before rounding the outside of the crosstrees and restarting the climb on the topmast shrouds proper. I could see that there were only three such shrouds, giving only two rungs for each ratline.

Looking further up, at and past the next set of futtock shrouds round the maintopmast crosstrees, I could see that for the last leg of the climb there were only two shrouds, narrowing to virtually nothing towards the top of the main topgallantmast, over eighty feet off deck. Put simply, the higher you climbed the less there was for feet to climb on and for hands to grip. As the number of shrouds holding the ratlines diminished, their stability decreased. And that was not the end of it. I would then have somehow to get myself off my narrow makeshift ladder on to the royal yard itself and work myself out the twelve feet or so from the mast to the yard end.

I understood by now that this was a test, and that the crew had gathered to see how I managed it and that it could determine the nature of my future aboard this ship. I knew that I would have to climb via the outside of the futtock shrouds. I had read enough sea-going literature to know that to take the inboard route through the inside of the crosstrees would mark me as a landlubber, if not a downright coward.

I looked aloft again and smiled, relaxing myself. The world around – the thunder clouds thickening overhead, the ship's crew gathered for what they hoped might be a bit of entertainment, the distant drone of traffic from the city, the downtown skyscrapers giving way to well-trimmed suburbs that finally transmuted to the endless miles of eucalyptus and swirling red dust stretching away to the heart of this hot and empty continent – receded and receded, sucked out of my consciousness until all that existed were those crystal clear shrouds and ratlines that now formed a simple and easy path to my goal at the starboard end of the main royal yard. Up I went without a concern in the world.

In general terms I don't have a great head for heights. I find they take a bit of getting used to. But that was the point. I was at that moment used to heights – very used to them. For over a year, not that long before joining *Endeavour II*, I had worked on the construction of high-rise buildings. All day, every day, I had been working at height, very often with nothing but a few four-by-two joists between me and the ground a hundred feet below. I had grown totally inured to any fear of height. It was just pure luck that the *Endeavour*

II had come along before that lack of fear had worn off.

So up I went, gaily swinging round the outside of the futtock shrouds, up the narrowing main topmast shrouds, round the outside of the two main topgallantmast futtock shrouds, on up to the royal yard, by which time the shrouds I was climbing were so close that my hands were almost touching. Then a leg off the shrouds on to the royal yard footrope, a wire in fact, one hand to grip the jackstay – the iron gripping bar running along the top of the yard. Transfer weight onto them and bring the other leg and hand over so that I was then firmly on the yard, supported by the footrope hanging four feet or so underneath, my hands gripping the jackstay. Then a sideways shuffle to bring me to the end of the yard.

All the way up I had kept totally concentrated on my climb, seeing nothing but my next handholds and footholds. Now I was there I let my vision once more expand, to take in and enjoy the view. Eighty feet below, the *Endeavour II* had become a toy ship, a convincing model with a row of tiny faces turned upwards to watch my progress. From here she looked much sleeker than from the quay, the deck planking accentuating her length. The deckhouses were now just flat mahogany rectangles seemingly set flush into the deck. To the west the city stretched away, disappearing into a moist haze under the grey cloud. Far inland the lightning of a summer afternoon thunderstorm flickered against a darker patch of sky. To the east I could now see round the bend of the river downstream of our mooring, and in the distance make out the wider expanses of Moreton Bay, the shallow inland waterway that leads to the Tasman Sea proper. That was the route the ship would have to take. I looked at the shackle holding the starboard brace. Tight as a drum and neatly wired. Surprise, surprise.

I regained the deck without any difficulty. *Shackle's*

OK, I said, handing the mate the spanner. *Yeah, well,* he replied, studying me quizzically with his hard eyes. *Yeah, well,* he said again, *I s'pose yer'll do. We're not working watches yet, apart from harbour watch. Report to Springer. He'll keep youse busy.* With a curt nod he stomped off aft.

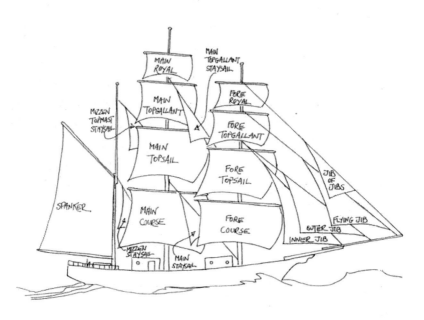

Endeavour II sail plan

5

The next few days were spent getting into the rhythm of shipboard life. As the ship was being prepared for sea, there was an endless succession of tasks. Mostly these fell into the category of 'marlinspike seamanship': splicing, whipping rope ends, worming, serving and parcelling areas of standing rigging where necessary, setting up the shroud tension by means of the dead-eyes, making baggywrinkle from old rope and renewing the anti-chafe gear. Brightwork was revarnished, ironwork was chipped down and repainted, the masts were slushed down with tallow so that the yards would raise and lower easily. The maintenance of a big sailing ship is a never-ending merry-go-round.

Most of the work was supervised by Springer, the bosun. Springer was a rigger by profession, and could do anything with rope or wire, practical or decorative, with an astounding facility. He was also an excellent and enthusiastic teacher. Within no time he had me doing Turk's heads and crown knots, Matthew Walkers and double diamonds. I learned how to make sennit, and how to weave an ocean plait. Under his guidance I made a ditty bag, to hold my seaman's tools – needles and palm, leather punch, spikes and so on. This had a leather base, made by soaking the leather until it was soft and pliable, then drying it out again over a mould to give a round base with the sides curling up an inch or so.

The canvas sides of the bag were then sown on to this base. Grommets were sown into the top of the bag to take the decorative draw-rope, tightened by a Turk's head. The construction of the bag used five different types of stitching, to represent the five oceans. The bag was later lost, and I have regretted it ever since.

As I worked I gradually got to know the rest of the crew. The ship's complement of fourteen were all young – a fairly even mix of adventurers from Canada, the USA, Australia, New Zealand and England. The skipper, Jeff Berry, an ex-US Navy mariner, was himself only twenty-eight years old. He was the antithesis of the dark-bearded glowering mate – tallish but unathletic, a bit podgy, with chubby red cheeks, blond hair and owlish spectacles. He was reserved and soft-spoken, cerebral rather than physical, academic rather than practical. I never managed to determine whether he really knew his stuff or not.

The mate we have already met, and the bosun, Springer. Springer had a guitar and a fund of sea shanties too, so was often the soul of our leisure time, as well as our work time. The bosun's mate, effectively number four in the chain of command, was the appropriately named Englishman Dave Salt. He was a brawny good-humoured West Countryman who knew his way around boats. The one female aboard, Vicki Watts, was also English, from Dorset. She was, I think, a trained nurse, but on *Endeavour II* she performed the normal duties of the 'foremast hand, same as the rest of us. She did, though, have her own private quarters.

As in any group, there were the characters who stood out. The 'baby' of the crew, though a good seaman, was the young Sydneysider Pete Duff, who had startled me on my first descent into the fore-peak; dreamy and hesitant under his mountain of unruly hair. We had our humorist, Jim 'Bones' Delaney, the ship's engineer, with his sharp wit and native

Kiwi talent for fixing anything with a 'bit of number eight fencing wire'. We had our own Olympic-class eater, too. The Canadian Rob Carey, one of the old hands who had been with the ship right across the Pacific, could consume mountains of food in record time, while staying as thin and lethal as the smile on a shark's lips. We were, in the main, a happy crew, devoted to the ship, keen that she should look her best. None of us had any money, so our entertainment was manufactured by ourselves, for ourselves, aboard the ship.

It would have been perfect but for my relationship with the mate. From the moment I had walked on board he had kept up a constant and insidious 'hazing' – subtle and not-so-subtle insults and put-downs. Orders to me were given in a curt, dismissive tone. In one sense that was his right. It was the tradition under sail that the mate should be something of a bully-boy, ready with his fists to knock the recalcitrance out of any wayward 'foremast hand. That was central to the fragile discipline of the square-rigged merchantman. But this was different. This was the late twentieth century. The skipper and the mate were first among equals, not unapproachable quarterdeck demi-gods. Moreover I knew pretty much what I was doing and worked hard. The mate too seemed to save up the worst of his tongue for me alone. Put plainly, it was unfair and unwarranted. It was inevitable that eventually I would react.

I can't remember the specific circumstance that sparked off my resistance to the mate's manner towards me. It was certainly late one evening, and we were in the galley. I think he had given me some order about the harbour watch I was to stand for some part of the coming night. Something about what he said, or the manner in which he said it, finally set off an explosive anger in me, that I could no longer contain. I knew this was another make or break moment aboard the ship. I may even have to leave it, but I knew that I had to sort this thing out then and there. There was no way I could allow his treatment of me to become an accepted norm.

I cannot recreate our exchange. I was so angry, and our initial argument so furious, that it would have been hard to remember exactly what was said even minutes afterwards. Basically I refused to do what he told me, and told him why. In general terms I told him, well, shouted at him, that the way he treated me was unacceptable; that I was ready and willing to do anything aboard this ship, but that I wouldn't put up with being constantly insulted, and singled out for bad treatment, for no good or apparent reason; that I respected the mate as a seaman but that I too needed a modicum of respect. All my pent up resentment came streaming out.

The mate's initial response, inevitably, was as loud and aggressive as mine. I do remember his first shouted words – *So whatcha gonna do 'bout it, eh? You wanna go on deck and fight about it? Of course not!* I shouted back, *What the hell would that prove?* Nevertheless, we were within an inch of going for each other, standing virtually toe to toe in our mutual anger. For a minute or two we traded verbal punches, mostly wild swings that achieved little but made us feel better.

The mate's tone became slightly more conciliatory. *I don't s'pose yer know that the sea-going watches have been drawn up, do you?* I shook my head. *Well they have, and you're on port watch. My watch. I selected you for my watch. All right? Just think about it, mate.* I reflected for a second or two and understood what he was getting at. It was his way of saying that he did in fact have some regard for my seamanship. The heat under our collars slowly evaporated. Our exchange became conversational in tone. For the first time, Chris talked to me in an almost friendly way. I had made my point, and Chris, it seemed, thought better of me for doing so. We parted that night on reasonably good, if still somewhat edgy, terms. I was never again subjected to gratuitous bullying.

6

Late in the afternoon of January 28th 1971 we hauled our mooring lines aboard and, with the ebb tide under us, motored down river under our small diesel engine. We were bound across the Tasman Sea to Auckland, New Zealand. We wound our way along the widening Brisbane River, past wharves, residential areas, industrial areas, jetties for this, jetties for that, the usual jumble of enterprise and aspiration thrown up on the shores of any sea-linked city. As the subtropical night fell, a bewildering vista of navigational lights, flashing white, red, or green, opened up ahead. It was not easy to tell their relative distance, nor how they charted the path through the shoals at the mouth of the river.

Our sea-going watch system had been set, with port watch, the mate's watch, keeping the deck from midnight until four on that first night. We were still motoring, feeling our way tentatively along the main channel. I was happy to remain on deck. I wanted to see it all and doubted if I could have slept much if I had turned in at midnight. At four in the morning, with most of the confusion of lights now falling astern, we were relieved by the starboard watch and went below. By the time I was warm in my bunk I was ready to fall into a deep sleep, lulled by the purring diesels.

Four hours later I was woken by the call for the change of watch. Something seemed different. The world had changed while we slept. Then I realised – the engines were stopped, we were lifting and falling to a swell, we must be sailing, and there, just inches from my ear, was the seductive gurgle of the bow wave rushing along the planking.

For a few seconds I closed my eyes again, and savoured the moment. It had all worked out. I really was here, able seaman on a unique and magnificent sailing ship, on the threshold of who knew what adventures. The music of the bow wave lured my imagination forward, on across the Tasman Sea, then away and up to the South Sea Islands, to pellucid lagoons fringed with shimmering coral, to long warm nights rocked gently beneath the wheeling Southern Cross, to island landfalls at the farthest ends of the earth. Every impossible boyhood dream was now within reach. Life could not have been better…

I came on deck and looked around. We were at sea. The land was now a thin grey line on the starboard quarter. The ship rose and dipped elegantly to the swells. We were heading south-east to our only projected stop on the voyage to New Zealand – Lord Howe Island. The ship had not been sailing for long. The starboard watch had set all our fore and aft canvas; jibs, staysails and the spanker, under which we were moving sedately with a moderate east-north-east wind just forward of the beam.

We breakfasted quickly, knowing that we would be soon sent aloft to loose the square sail gaskets. By then we had all spent so much time up in the rigging, preparing the ship for sea, that the prospect was not at all daunting. Nevertheless, even in the gentle sea that was running, we could see the huge arcs drawn in the sky by the mast trucks. There was no rush, the mate explained. *Take your time to get the feel of it and remember – one hand for the ship, one for yourself.*

One by one the courses, topsails and topgallants were

set. Three or four of us went aloft to loose the gaskets binding each sail to its yard. We quickly learned that there was no comparison between going aloft when moored alongside and going aloft at sea. In one sense it was easier, as the heel of the ship meant the ratlines were not so steep. On the other hand the motion at deck level was magnified by an increasing factor, the higher you went. Up there the masts described great circles in the sky, but they were not regular circles. Often a great swinging arc came to an abrupt stop, suddenly reversing the motion to the opposite direction. That was the danger point, when a poor grip could see you flung off the yard, or the ratlines you were climbing.

It was a lengthy process to set each sail, particularly with such a predominantly novice crew. For each sail the gaskets were first loosed. Then, on deck, the clewlines, buntlines and leechlines, used to haul the sail up to the yard, were cast off. The sail was sheeted home and the yard, apart from the fixed main yard, hauled up the mast. The yards were braced to the right angle to the wind, and cocked to the correct horizontal angle by means of the lifts. There were about twelve control lines for each sail. It meant finding the right ropes amongst the hundred and seventy or so pieces of running rigging belayed on the pin rails the length of the ship. All the hauling was manual. Prior to any manoeuvre all the lines to be used were 'capsized' – their coils taken off the belaying pins and thrown down on deck so that they would run freely. At the end of any manoeuvre the deck had to be 'made up' – every line neatly coiled and hung back on its belaying pin. Little surprise, then, that it took the best part of that four-hour watch to get the ship sailing properly under all square sail except royals.

We were bound for Lord Howe Island, several hundred miles off the east coast of Australia, and south-east of Brisbane. As the wind veered east we hardened the sheets and braced the yards as far forward as they would go. In moderate conditions *Endeavour II* could make some progress to windward – but not a lot. As with any square-rigger, the highest she could effectively sail was about six points off the wind. This gave, in modern sailing parlance, a tacking angle of about a hundred and thirty degrees. In rough conditions and high winds, the extra leeway meant windward progress was often impossible. We would soon learn this the hard way.

For the first few days out from Brisbane we had beautiful sailing weather, with clear skies and moderate winds. On the second day we were able to set the royals, the highest square sails. The ship, with its array of sails set from deck level to the mastheads, its maze of ropes criss-crossing in their individual tasks, was a stirring sight. Nine thousand square feet of canvas curved to the wind and sent us driving forward at eight knots or so. The ship came alive with its myriad sources of creaking and grinding and groaning, as the running rigging worked in its hundreds of squeaking blocks, ropes stretched and relaxed, frames and planking set up scores of infinitesimal but noisy rubbing points. The wind hummed its own medley of tunes through the tightly stretched miles of rigging, and the sea, breaking against our shapely bow and rushing aft, added its own darker counterpoint.

The ship was sailing beautifully, but with a leading wind only, and with the East Australian Current forcing us south, we could not lay a direct course to Lord Howe Island. On February 2nd we clewed up and furled the square sails, and started motoring east, to avoid a long and slow beat back to windward. As the next day broke there was Lord Howe Island ahead of us, its dramatic twin peaks backlit by blinding shafts of golden light from the rising sun. It could for all the world have been Papeete, or Nikuhiva, or maybe Easter Island...

Lord Howe Island, once a volcanic peak, has a beautiful lagoon, surrounded on two sides by towering cliffs, with a flatter area between making a third side. Unfortunately, our deep draft, at nearly fourteen feet, meant we could not cross the protective reef and anchor in sheltered water. We were forced to lie to anchor in the Southwest roads, with little protection and subject to the considerable oceanic swell. For three days we lay there, rolling diabolically, while we made fine adjustments to the rigging. Without a press of sail to dampen the motion aloft, working at height in the rig was simply hellish. The arc and ferocity of each roll, combined with the inescapable persistence of the motion, made even the simplest job quite unbearable.

We had a run or two ashore, but it was a long pull in the ship's gig. Lord Howe Island, apart from its magnificent scenery, had little to attract the shore-bound sailor. There was just one quiet hotel, which catered for honeymooning couples flown in by seaplane from Sydney, a few houses for the local residents, and that was it. We tried our luck chatting up the hotel waitresses and chambermaids, but it was an uphill struggle. We could not understand how indifferent these bored Sydney girls were to our super-charged masculinity. Surely we were manna from heaven? How could they resist such a bunch of sailors, so lean, so well-muscled, so bronzed, so...irresistible? As we were leaving, the one kind-hearted lass who, I must admit, had managed to overcome her evident revulsion enough to make the long row ashore and back to ship worthwhile, had the heart to whisper to me what the problem was. On board we used coconut oil soap, as it would lather up in seawater. We were used to its odd odour. They weren't. They had formed a unanimous opinion. We stank.

7

Heave! And heave! Heave! And heave! The mate's stentorian voice urged us on. At least ten of us were lined up in the waist of the ship, heaving and heaving on the fall of the big tackle rigged from the fore course yard. A Fish Burton Tackle, the skipper called it. It was his device for raising the anchor. For some strange reason, the *Endeavour II* had been built without a proper windlass. There was no mechanical system of any kind to raise the anchor. To hold us in the exposed anchorage off Lord Howe Island, our five hundred pound best bower anchor had been let go. It had held well, but we now had somehow to haul up a weight of nearly a quarter of a ton from the depths of the Tasman Sea, using nothing but blocks, tackles and our concerted muscle power.

It took six hours to get the damn thing up and properly catted. A few locals who had come out in their small boats to catch the rare sight of a square-rigger under full sail had long since abandoned the idea and returned to base. Once the anchor was clear of the bottom we had started to drift away to the south-east, farther and farther from the island, with not a stitch of sail set. It was an ignominious departure. By mid-afternoon the job was done, and with tired muscles from a day of hauling, we pulled ourselves aloft to loose the square sails and get properly under way.

There was one bonus from the hours of sweating – our

drift had brought us close to a wonder of the natural world – Ball's Pyramid. This is a thin needle of rock rising sheer and sharp out of the ocean to a height of nearly two thousand feet. It is a truly extraordinary sight: the startlingly symmetrical legacy of a chance succession of tectonic upheavals and watery erosions beyond imagining. We sailed close by, then set our course for the northern tip of New Zealand, just slightly south of east from our then position. Our next stop would be Auckland, some nine hundred nautical miles away.

The wind blew steadily from the north-east day after day, and we settled down to a proper sea-going rhythm. The watches came and went, four hours on, four hours off from eight at night until eight in the morning, with two six hour watches for the other twelve hours. This effectively rotated the watches every twenty-four hours. Everyone on board stood watch, except for the cook for the day. The ten able and ordinary seamen took turns to cook the three daily meals. On watch the helmsman was changed every hour. With seventeen sails to play with and adjust, it was usually possible to bring the ship to a more or less perfect balance, making her light and responsive to steer. With predominantly north-east winds we were mostly sailing full and bye on port tack, averaging about eight knots.

One day, for just a few hours, a fifteen-knot breeze came up from the south-west, on the starboard quarter, the ideal sailing wind. Luckily it coincided with our watch and I had the helm. After some discussion with the mate and some tweaking here and there, we got her as well balanced as possible and off she went at a comfortable twelve to thirteen knots. I have known no better or more thrilling sailing experience before or since. It was not simply the speed itself, which of course by modern standards was nothing exceptional. It was that this speed was being achieved with two hundred tons of sailing ship. It was the beauty and power of the sails and rig as they combined for their optimum performance. To have all that weight and power under one's fingertips, feeling it humming through the spokes of the wheel, was exhilarating beyond words.

However long or short a voyage, however benign or difficult the conditions, however much or however little must be done to keep a ship sailing, the crew of a sailing ship was always kept busy. Idleness was the breeding ground for discontent, so a sailorman was always made to work, work, work. What that work consisted of was often immaterial, all that mattered was that the crew be kept busy.

On the *Endeavour II* there was, likewise, always work to be done. Every morning, in good sailing ship tradition, the early morning watch holystoned the teak deck, keeping it sparkling white. Woe betide the hapless seaman who dropped oil or paint on it. Our regular dockside routine of constant rig maintenance carried on unchecked. Tarred twine was strung along the deck in rows, and old rope cut and teased apart to be woven into baggywrinkle on the twine. The hairy boa-like lengths of baggywrinkle thus manufactured were then taken aloft and wound round stays and shrouds, anywhere where there was a chance of chafe. Running rigging was constantly checked and ropes replaced or end-for-ended if too worn. Paintwork was kept fresh and sparkling. Blocks were stripped and oiled. On it went. The work was never-ending.

Off-watch, and on Sundays, the traditional rest day, we had plenty of fun and amusement. Our engineer, 'Bones' Delaney, was a fanatical fisherman. He fashioned a lure from an old spoon and promptly caught a four foot, fifty pound dorado. From time to time yellow-finned tuna were hauled aboard. In fine weather we rigged a bosun's chair on a block and tackle hung from the spanker boom. The lucky volunteer got himself firmly into the chair, which was then lowered to the surface of the sea, a few feet aft of the stern. To be thus dragged along, half in and half out of the water, at eight or ten knots, was as good as any fairground ride, and caused great hilarity amongst the onlookers gathered at the after rail. From time to time we 'showered'. The powerful seawater hose, driven by the diesels, was powered up and the jet played on the stripped down crew.

Off-watch, one could simply find a quiet spot aloft – the foretopmast top was my favourite, as the vista forward was unbroken, and one looked down the forestays along the luffs of the straining jibs to the bowsprit weaving its path forward – and watch the sea, the ever-changing sky and most of all, the beckoning horizon. Almost as good was simply to lie face down on the net strung beneath the bowsprit and watch the forefoot cutting its way through the waves. From time to time dolphins joined us, playing in packs just a few feet directly below. We sang too. On a lazy off-watch spell, particularly in the evening, we would sit on the poop deck, backs to the rail, and entertain ourselves and the helmsman with our growing repertoire of folksongs and shanties, taught to us by the irrepressible Springer.

After four days of steady fresh breezes we ran into a period of calms and light airs. We had once again been pushed well to the south and were struggling to get far enough north to round the two northern capes of New Zealand, Cape Reinga and North Cape. For a week we worked our way slowly and painstakingly north, in unhelpful, flukey winds. For a while an albatross adopted us. Masterful in the air, it became in the water an out-sized ungainly glutton, paddling behind the becalmed ship to pick, with its massive fluted bill, at any scraps thrown to it.

One night, in calm conditions, a red distress flare was spotted to the south. The sails were immediately clewed up and we set off under motor to investigate. We also radioed the New Zealand coastguard. We searched all night but found nothing. At first light a RNZAF Orion arrived to help the search. Apparently they spotted oil and some debris. No boat was ever reported missing and the mystery was never solved.

We resumed our voyage, clawing towards Cape Reinga. At last, eleven days out from Lord Howe Island, land was raised on the starboard bow. The north-west tip of New Zealand in fact has two capes, Maria van Diemen slightly to the south, then Reinga itself. For a while we used the motor once more to help us weather these capes and allow us to start the passage along the short northern coastline to North Cape. We were now well behind schedule for our arrival in Auckland, but the atmosphere on board ship was happy and relaxed. We worked well together as a crew, we were growing in skill and efficiency and we felt that the back of this voyage was broken. Land was again in sight. All that remained was to round North Cape and run down to Auckland, a straightforward and fast sail if we had the usual north-easterlies. Nothing could be simpler...

8

The tops and bottoms of islands and continents, the meeting points of seas and oceans, the bottlenecks where currents are forced in opposition, where the shoaling ocean floor, compressing the movement of trillions of tons of water, can throw the surface into massive turbulence – these are the dangerous oceanic nodes scattered around the globe that every sailor approaches with respect and circumspection. The great southern capes – Cape Horn, Cape Leeuwin and Cape Agulhas with its fierce eponymous current, the Pentland Firth, Bass Strait, the Dover Strait, Cook Strait; these spots, and a hundred more tucked away at all the world's marine interstices, have the capacity to create more than their share of trouble for the passing mariner.

The northern tip of New Zealand combines all the natural features of the born oceanic troublemaker. To the west the stormy waters of the Tasman Sea, its currents circulating anti-clockwise, and powered by the westerly stream of the Roaring Forties, force their way north and east. To the east lies the vast Pacific Ocean, where the trade winds blow predominantly from the east, setting up a drift opposed to the Tasman currents. The seabed off this northern tip is shallow, rising again to form the Three Kings Islands twenty miles or so to the north-west of the mainland. The mainland itself ends in an almost straight line of cliffs running due west to east for about twenty-five miles. The tides and currents run strongly, and the winds funnel along the cliffs.

As we rounded Cape Reinga, at the western end of the passage, we met the first signs of the trouble that lay ahead. Within the space of a few hours the wind was gusting to thirty knots out of the east and we started to meet, head on, the short, steep seas typical of a shallow tide race. The bowsprit was now regularly burying itself into the approaching wave faces, then throwing the sea off with wild skywards lurches. A couple of the braver hands of the starboard watch had the unenviable task of lowering and gasketing the flying jib, which meant a journey to the tip of the jibboom, lashing down the sail as they plunged into the waves.

We were now on starboard tack, close-hauled under reduced canvas and heeling heavily in the gusts as we drove awkwardly north-north-east. As the steeper waves passed under the ship we rolled to leeward, burying the deep bulwarks and half the deck. Lines were rigged along the deck to hang on to going fore and aft – a slip into the scuppers at the wrong moment could easily lead to an excursion overboard, quite probably for ever.

The conditions were too difficult to attempt to tack ship, so we wore round to start our first run south-east to weather North Cape at the eastern end of the passage. The steep seas and bucking motion of the ship were putting a severe strain on the rig, with the huge inertia of the heavy spars trying to tear the stays out of their fixings. That afternoon the fore topgallant-stay broke, threatening the foremast and taking our outer jib out of action. As we closed the line of cliffs we rigged a temporary rope stay. It was clear that on that tack we had no hope of rounding North Cape. We wore ship and once more headed north. The conditions were steadily deteriorating further, with gusts now up to thirty-five knots.

By this time the mate, Chris Scott, was not at all happy. We had been brought in closer than he would have liked to the rocky coastline before turning north again. Over the weeks at sea I had developed a growing respect for Chris as a sailor. He was undoubtedly a hard nut, and had crewed and navigated on many ocean-racing yachts, but he nonetheless had a careful and defensive attitude to ship handling under sail. His neat and meticulous navigation belied his tough exterior. As we tacked north again it was clear that a disagreement was developing between him and the skipper. The skipper was under pressure to deliver the ship to Auckland in time for the Cook celebrations, of which we were to form the centrepiece. We were running out of time, after a relatively slow passage from Brisbane, and he wanted to press on. The mate, by contrast, was increasingly worried about our position in this worsening weather, and had advised the skipper that we should keep standing on north to get well clear of land to ride out the storm that was evidently coming. We were at that stage not yet fully aware of it, but what was developing was the classic conflict between the schedules and demands of daily life on land, and the quite different rhythms and imperatives of nature itself.

The difference of opinion between the officers was not overt – they had the good sense to try to keep a lid on it in front of the crew, but in such a small closed group, living cheek by jowl, nothing could be disguised for long, and it was soon no secret. The mate was, of course, in a difficult position in regard to disagreeing with the skipper. To advise and perhaps to argue a different point of view, in a reasonable manner, would be acceptable. To openly disagree would amount to insubordination – a direct challenge to the skipper's authority. That authority, virtually absolute, is enshrined in maritime law and tradition. The skipper's word is law, full stop, end of story. Any more junior officer who forgot or ignored that would risk his career.

That night the skipper's watch had the deck from midnight to four in the morning. They wore ship and once more headed south in the second attempt to weather North Cape. Below, sleep came, but only through habit and extreme tiredness. Up in the forepeak bunks we were having a wild ride as the prow of the ship rose and plunged every few seconds. The planking shuddered as each wave slammed into us. Jets of water squirted through the seams as the planks worked, loosening the caulking. Each watch was now pumping regularly to clear the well.

By daylight, for the second time, we were bearing down on the Cape and its rocky outposts. All hands were called, in case a sudden manoeuvre was necessary. The mate was visibly distressed at our proximity to the cliffs, now growing increasingly ominous as the weather worsened further. In the driving spray and rain they loomed black and cold and immutable. At the last moment, the skipper having accepted that we could not pass to windward, we wore ship and once more clawed off the coast to the north.

It was as well now that we had been at sea for three weeks or so, and had our sea legs well established. The wind had stepped up a gear in intensity and we had to reduce sail further. To go aloft now, to furl the topgallant sails, was a different order of challenge to anything we had so far faced. The ship's motion in the increasingly angry and hollow seas was magnified to wild gyrations at sixty feet above deck. The heeling of the ship to the gale brought the yards over the sea at a steep angle, making it much more difficult to maintain good footholds and handholds. The driving rain blinded us and made every surface slippery. *One hand for the ship and one hand for yourself...* But to haul the heavy canvas up to the yard and pass and tie gaskets, in that weight of wind, could not be done with one hand alone. To have two hands available for the job meant pushing the foot-rope out aft and lying horizontally across the yard, gripping as best one could with one's stomach. It was a dangerous and precarious position, but there was no alternative.

Later that morning the main topsail tore in the heavy wind, and that too had to be furled. The reduction of sail continued with the reefing of the spanker. We were now down to courses, fore topsail, spanker and inner jib. In one sense *Endeavour II* was revelling in the conditions, averaging five knots or so through the water, despite being hard on the wind into enormous cliff-like seas. We were moving relatively fast, but not making enough progress where it counted – to windward.

At midday we once more wore ship and headed south for our third attempt to weather North Cape. The wind had backed slightly to north-east, giving us a better slant on our southerly board. However it also meant that if we did succeed in passing the Cape the gale, still growing in intensity, would be absolutely square to the coastline, which from North Cape runs to the south-east. We would be wilfully putting ourselves directly to windward of a lee shore. The skipper, despite the days it had taken us to beat the relatively few miles from Cape Reinga to North Cape, still seemed to retain an overly optimistic view of the ship's windward ability in these conditions. Perhaps he believed what he wanted to believe or what he felt he had to believe. He was convinced that, once past North Cape, our problems would be over. An objective assessment of the chart, the conditions, and our performance so far, could well have argued otherwise.

On the afternoon of 19th February 1971 the *Endeavour II*, twenty-two days out from the Brisbane River, and after nearly a week of beating to windward in storm conditions that had not yet reached their full fury, weathered the North Cape of New Zealand. In so doing she put herself in mortal danger. A trap, as old as man's first halting attempts to sail the oceans, lay waiting patiently for another victim. Once past the Cape, the jaws began to close. There would be no escape.

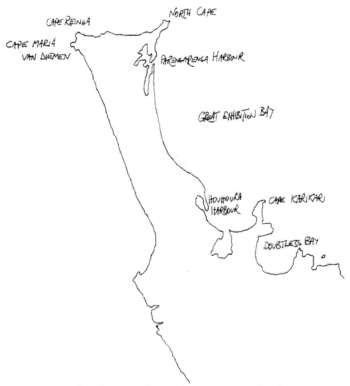

Sketch map of Northern New Zealand

9

Tropical storms start in the low latitudes to the north or south of the equator. The warm late-summer seas send up moist air into the upper atmosphere. If there is not too much wind at that height the moisture condenses, creating energy and heat that draws up more air. A great vertical system of circulating air starts to form. The rotation of the earth adds to the effect, spinning the system to the north east or south east, depending on the hemisphere, away from the equator. If the energy generated reaches a powerful enough level, whipping the circulating air currents to fantastic speeds around a calm eye, a hurricane is born.

Hurricane, typhoon, tropical cyclone – different names: same thing, same result – mayhem. What was bearing down on the *Endeavour II*, as she struggled past North Cape, was not, fortunately, a full hurricane, but was nonetheless a weather system of the next intensity down – a tropical storm. Meteorologists normally define this as a low-latitude gener-ated storm with winds between thirty-five and sixty-five knots. In the Beaufort Scale of measurement this equates to Force 8 to 10. This is not the sort of weather that a sailor likes to meet at any time. To meet it in a square-rigged ship, with land just a few miles to leeward, scarcely bears contempla-tion.

Once past North Cape we battled on south-eastwards,

close-hauled on port tack. The wind now got up with a real vengeance, moaning relentlessly in the rigging and driving sheets of blinding spray and rain across the wave tops. The world closed around us in a grey disembodied shroud. By late afternoon, through the spume-laden air ahead, we made out the black cliffs of the next headland down the coast – the headland whose weathering was now becoming, quite literally, a matter of life or death – Cape Karikari. The headland was fine on our port bow. We were already too far to leeward. The door, already firmly shut behind us, was now shutting ahead. There was no option but to wear ship, losing more precious sea room, and head back north.

This was a devastating blow. The skipper had, according to murmurs passed along from the starboard watch, been confident that there would be no more obstacles to our progress down the coast, and that our next close encounter with the mainland would be at Cape Brett, the easterly headland at the south entrance to the Bay of Islands. The conditions were forcing us to leeward at a far greater rate than anticipated, pinning us closer and closer to an unwelcoming and invisible shore.

As we bore north again, watching the high rocky outcrop that barred our progress recede once more into the darkening haze astern, a pall fell over the ship. For the first time it was clear to everyone on board, down to the least experienced novice, that there was no longer any basis for pretence or misplaced optimism. However much we smiled bravely at each other and cracked tense, devil-may-care jokes, there was no hiding the stark truth – our position was rapidly becoming critical.

The deliberations between the skipper and the mate were now curt, tense, vitriolic. The mate was furious that we had been put in this position against his advice. The skipper clung to his it'll-all-be-fine attitude of denial; an attitude that was quickly eroding his capacity for realistic decision-making. On the coast to leeward there was one possible refuge, Houhora Harbour, at the south-west corner of the bay in which we were trapped, Great Exhibition Bay. However, its entrance would be difficult to pinpoint, particularly in such poor visibility, in the uniform line of cliffs and hills that would confront us. As we raced in with a following wind and sea, there would be little time or ability to adjust our course. The consequences of an error, that would drive us straight at storm-battered precipices, were all too clear. We kept on north, now working desperately to maximise every inch to windward.

All night we reared and plunged our way back towards North Cape. The cold and wet, combined with the days and days of forcing the ship into these heavy seas, were slowly sapping the young crew of its energy and optimism. As each day passed, with its endless rhythm of watch and watch about, with its constant struggles and tussles with heavy canvas and ropes stretched to breaking point, and with its incessant rising and falling and lurching and rolling that made every task a muscle-draining balancing act, the world we had known, the simple world on land where everything was mostly neat and dry and stable and predictable, receded into some unattainable dream-like realm somewhere there beyond the storm-whipped horizon. This was now our sole universe. We were now a race apart, clinging to our ninety feet of heaving deck, united in our fate, blood brothers by chance. There was no exit, no getting off. We had not meant it to be like this, but it was, and that was that.

The next morning broke as we now felt it always would, with the rain still machine-gunning our raw cheeks, and the wind still whining its relentless litany of destruction. Yet again we wore ship for another attempt to weather Cape Karikari to the south-east. The wind howled out of the north-east, never changing direction. It was only a wind shift that could now give us the key to unlock the manacles that were binding us closer and closer to an impending disaster. Just a point or two one way or the other was all that was needed. After over a week of flukey variable winds in the eastern Tasman, it seemed cruel that the storm had locked itself immutably into the one narrow vector that would destroy us. On it blew, harder and harder, forcing the seas into massive combers, with never a degree's variation in its direction. We were pinned ineluctably to the land behind, a helpless butterfly skewered on a collector's board. After another wretched day crashing south, night came with no sign of land. Where exactly we were was a matter of dead reckoning over a long period in mind-numbing conditions. In other words no more than a desperate guess.

Lookouts were set at the foremast top, as well as the usual bow. At the change of the evening watch Cape Karikari light was finally sighted. In one sense this was good news – we could re-establish our position with certainty. Otherwise the news was bad. The light, and the Cape that bore it, were once again on our port bow. For more than twenty-four hours we had ridden the ship as hard as we dared to windward and were now back almost exactly where we had begun. For the second time we wore away from Cape Karikari to the north, retracing our previous tracks, but in parallel, always that bit closer to the unseen dangers under our lee.

The ship had certainly never known such hard use, and in the cold light of the next morning the constant pounding started to take its toll. The fore topmast back-stay ripped out its chain-plate. This immediately allowed the fore topmast a dangerous amount of movement, which in its turn caused further damage to the attachments for the fore topmast fut-tock shrouds. A jury back-stay was immediately rigged, but the fact was that the fore topmast was now out of action. This meant that we could no longer carry the fore topsail, always one of the most important storm sails on a square rigger, or any of the sails above that. The fore topsail was quickly and roughly furled, and the fore course set in its place.

We were now sailing under just three sails – the inner jib, fore course and mizzen staysail. It was not reasonable to expect this small spread of sail to drive two hundred tons of ship, hampered by the huge windage of its complex rig, to windward. Perhaps the skipper realised this, as he then made one last desperate, wildly optimistic bid to force our way past Cape Karikari, and into the shelter that could possibly be found in Doubtless Bay to the south west of the cape. He decided that we would try and motor our way past.

It was a hopeless, last-ditch proposition. The small diesel could no more take us straight up into the wind and power us head on into the great swells than could our canvas. As we plunged into each trough the stern came clear of the water, leaving the propeller to claw the air uselessly before the bow was picked up by the next wave and thrown backwards. Maybe we could have just about have held station against the elements, maintaining our position and buying time, the precious time before conditions changed which, by the immutable laws of nature, they eventually must. However our supplies of fuel were already low, reduced by the considerable unscheduled use of the engine in the eastern Tasman. At dusk that night, as we wallowed for the third time at a spot just to the north-west of Cape Karikari, way short of rounding it, the engine coughed apologetically for the last time and, for a moment, the ship went deathly silent.

No more roar and scream of the diesel revving to its near maximum to force us forwards straight into the bared teeth of the storm; no more whining of propeller cutting air instead of water. Just a sudden and awful silence that gripped our hearts as we heard nothing and knew what it signified... no more hope. That silence, for its first few shocking seconds, spoke as eloquently as the sounds that turn a man's bowels to water – the hissing of the guillotine blade as it starts its irrevocable descent; the clicking release of the firing squad safety catches, the singing and whistling of the cold and finely-tempered blade as it arcs down to the warm flesh and pulsing blood resting on the block beneath. All sound and fury had drained away and left a great vacuum of nothingness that filled our heads, suspending us for a moment in time as we confronted, each in our own way, the truth that was surely inevitable – nothing could save us now. The engine died, and with it died too the last fluttering pulses of unreasonable optimism.

10

We bore off north once again into the howling black night, once more under inner jib, fore course and mizzen staysail. Port watch had the deck until midnight. I was flattered to be asked by the mate to take the helm, with quiet instructions to keep her up to windward as much as was humanly possible, without losing way and without, worse still, getting caught aback. It was a vote of confidence that put to rest once and for all our earlier disagreement.

The foremast steaming light had been switched on to illuminate the headsail luff and make it easier to sail the best course possible. I was glad to have something very specific to do and concentrate on. I was soaked throughout and chilled to the bone, but that no longer seemed of any relevance. My eyes never left the jib luff, a hundred feet or so ahead of me in the ethereal, disembodied glow of the steaming light. I relaxed to the rhythm of the waves, bearing off a shade now and again to keep her driving into the steeper wave faces, but always coming back as close as I could to the wind to grab every available yard to windward. With a task to do, and the comforting mahogany spokes of the huge wheel under my frozen fingertips, my fear, for a while, ebbed away.

The mate was in and out of the chartroom, checking our speed and course and drift, and calculating, calculating. What he calculated was not good. The land was now just a few miles ahead on our lee bow. The skipper had no strategy but to sail on. There was little choice. The mate now seemed resigned to the frustrations of his position. Having seen the course of events since he tried, but failed, to influence the decision-making of the skipper, he had assumed the persona of the dogged second-in-command, doing everything required of him and executing the orders of the skipper with a quiet but broody deference.

On we sailed, the crew on deck tense, silent and near exhaustion after a week of debilitating struggle against the storm. The wind kept on its ceaseless blast out of the north-east, never wavering. We knew the end-game must now be near. We were simply running out of sea room. Soon there would be no more water in which to navigate. We would hit land.

For a week, on and off, we had been observing the uncompromising cliffs and rock that, to us at least, were the New Zealand coastline. Close in on many occasions, we had seen the surf pounding the black bases of the cliffs, creating a maelstrom of white foam, and throwing up great showers of spray so high they seemed to merge with the scudding low clouds above. Nobody ever voiced the thought, but every one of us well knew that to run ashore onto a remote and sheer cliff face, with no possibility of any aid, on a wild black night in storm force winds and in monstrous seas that had been building for a week, was simply not survivable. Fourteen young minds contemplated their imminent deaths, and the manner of their dying.

At midnight our watch was relieved. I struggled forward along the heaving deck and down the hatchway into the noisome dark of the forepeak and into my water-logged sleeping bag. Fitful sleep came and went. I did not dare sleep, but all the same craved a deep oblivion of escape, and so drifted back and forth between semi-wakefulness, sub-consciously listening out for and analysing the sounds from the deck above, and heavy uneasy bouts of deeper sleep...

All hands on deck and bring your lifejackets! The words force themselves through my shell of semi-consciousness. They reverberate in my unwilling head, that knows already what they mean but that, for just one heartbeat, attempts to ignore them, to forget them, to pretend they never existed. Not possible. It is not possible to ignore them. Nor is it possible to ignore their meaning, nor their implication. There is no escaping them. At the second heartbeat I am fully awake, and my stomach lurches. This, I know, is finally it.

I leaped out of my bunk, and with shaking fingers pulled on my oilskin and tied the tapes of my lifejacket. The ship was lurching erratically, in sympathy with my innards. I struggled up through the hatch onto the sloping fore-deck and froze rigid. The foremast light illuminated a semi-circle of sea around the bows of the ship. The sea was an angry mass of churning white water.

I had one single, paralysing thought. Rocks. We are driving onto rocks. For several seconds I could not move. My muscles seized. I experienced, for the first time in my life, the true meaning of the word *petrified*. In all but the most literal sense my body turned to stone; cold, rigid, locked into a statuesque attitude of terror. My stunned brain summarised the position. We were on rocks, we would in short order be pounded to bits and within who knows how many minutes or hours I would be dead. I was twenty-three years old. I did not want to die. I did not want to be smashed to a bloody rag-doll on this foreign shore. This cannot be happening.

Through the fog of wailing, tumbling thoughts that clouded all my senses, I realised that somewhere there was a voice, yelling furiously. Rob Carey, of the starboard watch, was screaming at me to help him. He was desperately trying to lower the inner jib, which was flogging and snapping violently in the still-furious gale, and needed an extra hand to tail on the down-haul. For another second I still could not move. Rob screamed at me again to get forward and help him. I snapped out of my frozen immobility and leaped forward to grab the down-haul and start heaving. As soon as I got working I felt better. It was unlikely that there could be any escape from an imminent death, but I would fight it all the way. My anger at the seeming unfairness of it all found an outlet as I hauled frantically on the taut rope, helping bring the now redundant sail down to deck level.

The ship heaved up as a huge swell passed underneath, and slewed sideways through the boiling water with a dull thump. Then again. As we worked to smother and lash down the heavy canvas of the jib, my gaze kept wandering to the lit-up patch of sea around us, looking for the black backs and razor fins of the rocks that would kill us, and expecting any moment to see a wall of cliff appear in the gloom to leeward. No rocks came, nor any cliff.

The ship, which had been heeled heavily to port, suddenly came upright. The sea in an instant became eerily calm, and the white water that had been churning around us was now black and smooth and still. The masts and rigging still wailed with the sound of the gale, but the ship was strangely peaceful. For the first time in over a week we were not hobby-horsing our way into the storm-driven seas, but drifting sideways in water so relatively tranquil that it could have been the Serpentine on a Sunday afternoon.

A party under the command of the skipper had let go the starboard bow anchor. A second sheet anchor had also been heaved overboard but the cable had parted. During the setting of the anchors the skipper's right wrist had been broken. The port anchor too was prepared and let go. As far as we could tell the anchors were holding. The ship did not appear to be taking water, despite the heavy bumps she had experienced. We were in calm water, evidently in the lee of a sandbank or perhaps a bar, across which we appeared to have been carried. Where exactly we were was anyone's guess.

Nobody turned in again that night. It had been about an hour after the midnight change of the watch when we had first grounded. By two in the morning at the latest we were swinging to anchor in our strange refuge. The rest of the night was spent clearing up the decks and re-gasketing the sails that had been hurriedly dropped when we struck. There was palpable relief amongst the crew. We had all thought our last moments had come, but here we were, seemingly safe after all. It seemed miraculous. A few tentative jokes were cracked but our hearts weren't in them. We still were not sure where we were, or whether any further trials or dangers lay ahead. It was as well we did not relax too much. Our ordeal was by no means over. In fact it had hardly begun.

11

Parengarenga Harbour is a remote and extensive inland sea situated just a few miles south of the north-east tip of New Zealand's North Cape. Its shores and banks are sandy, and, in those days at least, it was an important source of sand for the New Zealand construction industry. The sand was dredged up and carried by barge to the cities further south. The area is sparsely populated. Tidal waters flow in and out of the harbour through a channel a mile or so long and half a mile wide. The tides are big, and a huge volume of water is forced in through the channel, then pours out again on the ebb. To the south of the channel entrance a long sandy spit, dividing the harbour from the sea, stretches away to the south. The coast north of the channel entrance takes up the more usual New Zealand theme of rocky outcrops and high cliffs leading up to North Cape itself, five miles or so further north.

As the ebony shroud of night slowly turned to charcoal and then grey, and the features surrounding us took on a distinguishable form, we realised what an extraordinary chance sequence of events had spared us almost certain destruction the night before. Our anchors had brought us to rest absolutely dead centre of the channel leading into Parengarenga Harbour. Seawards we could see the huge combers breaking on the bar that guards the entrance. A conjunction of a high enough tide and big enough swells had enabled the ship to be carried bodily across the bar, grounding as she went, but not hard enough to open her up.

The *Endeavour II* drew about fourteen feet. We later learned that the maximum water on the bar was about nine feet. In all but the most extreme conditions we could never have crossed it in the way that we did. If we had stuck the night before, which was certainly the most probable outcome, the ship would have been smashed to pulpwood there and then. The chances of survival of any of the crew would have been absolutely minimal. Had we managed to keep the ship further to windward, and kept at sea longer before striking, then we would have piled up on the rocky cliffs to the north. I reflected ruefully on this as I thought about my efforts the previous evening to grab as much to windward as I could. A better performance would have meant our destruction. To the south lay a stretch of sandy coastline. Had we struck earlier there is no question the ship would have been lost there and then. There may have been a marginally better chance of survival amongst the crew, but that would have depended as much as anything on the tides and currents prevailing when the ship broke up. All in all we had been incredibly lucky. Our lives, that had seemed poised to enter the dark and unknowable abyss, had been restored to us.

We had been in radio contact with the New Zealand coastguard service since finally failing to weather Cape Karikari. A tug had put out from the northern port of Mangonui, to the south of Cape Karikari, but had turned back with a smashed wheelhouse. A small launch had tried to get fuel to us from inside Parengarenga Harbour, but it had suffered engine failure and been carried back by the flood tide into the harbour. New Zealand Search and Rescue had considered the possibility of helicopter assistance, but concluded it was 'virtually impossible' with such low cloud, rain and high wind. Every avenue of assistance was blocked. We were on our own.

Mid-morning the tide turned. Up until then we had been lying reasonably quietly, head to wind and tide, but as the ebb tide, emptying millions of tons of water out of the harbour through the narrow channel, started to pick up strength, conditions changed. A six-knot tide against a forty-knot wind is a sure-fire recipe for throwing up a short sea. Inevitably the ship started to pitch and roll, snubbing at her anchors. Even worse, the ebb tide, its force acting on our long deep keel, was trying to lever the ship round, while the wind, throwing its weight at our spars and rigging and topsides, was pressing us back the other way. We were caught fair and square between the opposing forces. The result was that we were now presenting our maximum lateral area to the ebb tide. In the tug of war between wind and tide, the tide had the upper hand. The bottom was soft, shifting sand. It was too soft for our anchors to bite into properly.

Slowly and inexorably we moved seawards once again, as the anchors dragged on the poor holding. With horror we realised what was happening – we were being pushed back, against the gale, towards the sand bar that we had so miraculously crossed the night before. We were caught in the iron grip of the elements, with no fuel, damaged rigging, an exhausted crew, an injured skipper, and no possibility of external aid. As the tide rushed out, lowering the depth of water over the bar, we could see the breakers tumbling ever steeper and more destructively. Once more the atmosphere on board changed to one of grimness. We were collected in the waist of the ship, wondering if any *deus ex machina* would again intervene to pluck us from the jaws of catastrophe. At least it was day-time. We could see where we were. That gave some comfort. The thundering of the surf on the bar came closer. There was no question. We were heading straight for it.

The first intimations that we were once again grounding were almost benign, a few gentle nudges as if from an inquisitive whale. We looked at each other in silence, recognising now that there could be no intervention. We were going to be carried into the maelstrom of breakers just a stone's throw to windward. What that would mean for us, for the ship, we did not dare contemplate. There was now nothing we could do about it. We had struggled so hard for so many days that our stoicism was honed to an indestructible edge. We would just take whatever comes, and be damned.

The gentle nudges of the keel on the sand beneath grew more urgent, more meaningful. The tide was still pushing us into shallower water, and every few yards gave more scope to our rise and fall. As the ship came down harder the nudges became thumps, hard, dull-edged, prophetic. Still we moved seawards into whiter and whiter water. Each wave passing under us lifted the two hundred tons of ship, then seemed to pause for a second. We knew what was coming, and each time it grew more unbearable. We were held at the top of the crest for that tantalising moment, then dumped downwards on to the sand beneath. The thumps as we hit the sand were now great solid mortar-bomb thuds.

We had by now collected on the poop deck aft, to be as clear as we could from any danger from falling spars. We were now about two miles out to sea. On the sands to the south of the harbour entrance we could make out the shape of a Land Rover and a small group of people. Cold comfort. Up until now the breakers had just been toying with us, just giving us a gentle taster of their power. As the tide ebbed further each regular assault on the ship grew to terrifying intensity. Each wave seemed to pick her up higher and contemptuously hurl her down harder on her keel. Each crash on to the sand was now a heavy artillery explosion, sending shock waves of vibration through every timber of the ship.

Crouched on the after deck we could see the stern post forcing up the teak planking a foot or two each time the rudder cannoned into the sand. The foremast, already weakened, was now tottering dangerously. The mate reported that the radio was now out of action. The ship was taking water and the batteries were flooded. We knew now there was no hope. The ship was being smashed open. She would never float again.

Again and again we lifted up to the breakers, then thudded sickeningly on to the sand. It was heart-breaking to feel such a rare and beautiful craft being destroyed beneath us. No vessel could withstand this sort of assault for long. Our own position was becoming critical too. For the moment we had a platform to cling on to, but for how long would it hang together? We had taken lines round our waists and lashed ourselves to the rail to avoid being swept off. For an unbearable hour we pounded, feeling the life ebb out of the ship. As she filled with water she rose more sluggishly to the crests and gradually canted over on her starboard side, deck and masts away from the murderous combers; a sick, dying leviathan.

I thought it was not possible to endure anything worse than that relentless pile-driving on to the hard sand. I was wrong. As the tide continued to ebb and the waterlogged ship settled on the bar, the changed configuration brought on a step change to the power and manner of the onslaught. The lifting of the ship to the waves had been giving us some protection from them. We were, as it were, riding to the punches. Now that the ship had become an unmoving obstacle, the waves simply broke right over the hull.

For the first time we started to feel the full force of the breakers ourselves as tons of water reared up over the ship and cascaded down onto our puny backs. We were now in serious danger of simply being swept off our sloping refuge into the sea. We doubled our lashings and gripped limpet-like on to anything firmly attached as each new wave dumped its mass of solid water onto us. The after rail was smashed. We were regularly sent slithering down the deck in a cascade of flailing limbs. We lashed ourselves together. The great hills of water kept on coming and coming, scouring our raw flesh as they ripped over us, tearing at our life-blood, beating us to submission.

From time to time we had thrown floating objects, mainly old lifejackets, over the side, to gauge where we would be carried if we were forced into the water. Always the answer was the same – straight out to sea, and quickly. The great inner harbour was still emptying itself, driving the rapid ebb stream past us and out to the deeper water beyond. Our survival was becoming a matter of timing. Would the ship break up before the tide turned? Would we be swept off by the power of the waves before the tide turned? Was our fate to be driven off and out to sea, to drown or freeze in the misnamed waters of the Pacific?

12

Shivering with cold, battered and bedraggled, cowering from the surf, we clung on and waited. The receding tide now gave some relief from the breakers – there was less water on the bar and the waves were marginally less threatening. The ebb tide could not last forever, that we knew. Yet another unneeded lifejacket was flung overboard, yet again it was carried seawards. The combers battered the hull, but fewer waves were passing right over the top, onto us. In the occasional lulls, huddled round the after deck, we discussed our position. We could not stay much longer where we were. The ship would surely not withstand the onslaught that would build up again after the tide had turned and a depth of water built up again on the bar. Nor would we. It was now after midday, so there would be daylight for a good few hours more.

There seemed to be little choice. Once the tide turned we would have to abandon ship and entrust ourselves to the surf. With the onshore gale, still howling unabated, and the flood tide, we should be carried shore-wards. Where we would fetch up, and how long it would take, and what conditions would be like adrift in the water, were unanswered questions. The ship had a twelve-man life-raft. We could squeeze into that. It may not be so bad. We still had to be very careful. The skipper no longer had the use of his right arm. Vicki Watts could not swim. It would be an easy matter to lose someone in the rough and tumble of the surf. Even getting everyone safely into the life-raft would not be straightforward. Another lifejacket went overboard, and for the first time, did not race off seawards. At last, at last, we were at slack water. The murderous ebb tide, author of all our recent suffering, ultimate destroyer of our ship, had run its course.

For another thirty minutes we waited, to be sure the current had turned towards the land. The large life-raft canister was manhandled to the poop deck, ready to be launched overboard. Another spare lifejacket was despatched over the side. It set off purposefully to leeward, towards the shore. The moment had come to abandon ship. The skipper checked with all the crew that they were in agreement. Not surprisingly there were no dissenters. The prospect of going over the side into the boiling maelstrom was hardly attractive, but to remain on board now would mean certain destruction.

The end of the long rope lanyard that attaches to the life-raft and triggers the self-inflation mechanism was lashed firmly to the ship. We lifted the heavy canister and flung it overboard into the seething white water to leeward. Caught immediately by the flood tide and the wind the canister raced away. It would be brought up short by the lanyard and would inflate. We would then haul it back alongside. So went the theory. The canister raced away unchecked. The mate hauled in the lanyard to its bitter end. It had pulled out of the canister. Stunned, we stared at the lanyard end with its wire trace, now hanging limply in the mate's hand. The life-raft was gone. A minute later, a hundred or so yards from the ship, an orange canopy opened up in the surf to leeward. The life-raft had inflated itself.

Grim and disbelieving, we watched our rescue craft drift

off until it was lost to view in the heavy seas. It had been heading straight for the main shore a couple of miles away where the Land Rover was parked – the ideal spot. That it had gone without us, failed us at our one moment of incalculable need, was almost too much to bear. Would there be no end to our misfortune?

Maybe, but we were not beaten yet. The ship had a second inflatable, just a large rubber dinghy. It was no longer useable as a proper life-raft, as the bottom had already been ripped out by the force of the gale. It was now just a big inflated rubber ring, lashed to the roof of the galley. It would have to do. It was all we had that would keep everyone together in the water and give some support to the injured, the non-swimmers, the poor swimmers and the exhausted.

Struggling on the sloping deck, and fighting to stop the light rubber being torn from our grasp by the screaming wind, we unlashed it and dragged it aft. A plan of action was quickly agreed. We were crouched in a line inside the smashed after rail. Firstly we checked that everyone was firmly roped to the person in front of them in the line. It was imperative that no-one should be separated from the main party. Our only hope and strength lay in keeping closely together, supporting each other physically and mentally. The plan was that we would go over the side one by one, each taking a position round the outside of the ring, hanging on with one arm, until all fourteen of us were arrayed around it. The rope holding the ring to the ship would then be cast off, consigning us to the whim of the elements.

Over the side we went. As each crewmember dropped over the lee rail into the water below, the line moved along, keeping us all still attached together. Slowly a circle formed around the rubber ring. The tail of waiting crewmembers still aboard got shorter and shorter. My turn came to leave the ship forever. I dropped down into the sea and was surprised to feel the sand under my feet. At low tide there was only four or five feet of water on the bar. Having a footing made it easier for us to arrange ourselves as symmetrically as we could around the ring. In the immediate lee of the ship we had some shelter from wind and waves, and so were able to prepare ourselves for the next ordeal in a relatively orderly way. A final check was made that everyone had a good grip on the ring. The slip rope holding us to the ship was let go and, slowly at first, we started to move away from the stricken hull.

We had no notion of what to expect as we drifted away from the shelter of the ship. There was no going back. Our fate was totally down to the current that was gradually acting on us. The life-raft had seemed to head for the beach, but there was no guarantee that we would follow it. With its high canopy and light weight, the life-raft was more subject to the strong onshore wind than the current. We were a heavy mass well down in the water, fourteen torsos, twenty-eight flailing legs, bound together by rope and a thin rubber membrane. We would go where the water took us, not the wind. What if there was a strong southerly set to the flood tide, once we got into the deeper water to the lee of the bar? Would we just be carried along parallel to the shore, a mile or two away? Would we just keep on drifting through the surf, unable to paddle or in any way direct such an ungainly craft, until exhaustion and cold and hopelessness finally claimed us one by one?

Down there in the water, with as yet small waves already starting to break over our heads, leaving us gasping and spluttering, the world took on a different perspective. The land had gone, invisible behind the high swells downwind. All we could occasionally glimpse of *Endeavour II* were the masts and yards, angled crazily towards us, and now disappearing behind each advancing crest. The solid comfort of the teak deck was gone forever. Our hold on the world was now at its most tenuous. The sea, always beckoning, always so enticing, now had us in its icy grasp. As we fought in the increasing surf to keep our mouths and noses clear of the water, our universe now just a few yards of steely water and a circle of bobbing heads and elbows crooked to keep some hold on the rubber ring, it was hard not to believe we would succumb. It would be so easy. The sea was so cold. We were so tired. We were so drained by these days and days of relentless effort. For what? Why fight? Why bother? The sea is so cold. Why bother? Why fight? It would be so easy. Why fight? For what? The sea is so cold. It would be so easy to give up the struggle, to gently release one's grip and slide gratefully into the embrace of mother sea…

The first huge breaker of the deeper water picked us up and hurled us flailing into the trough. We started shouting at each other. *Everyone OK? Everyone got a grip? Anyone need any help?* The will to live sparked once more. Vicki was struggling to keep going. From time to time she appeared to pass out in the water. We made sure she was well supported on each side. The violence of the surf, now curling and breaking fully as we drifted into open water, threw up yet more unspoken questions. How long would we be able to maintain our grip on the ring if things got worse? How much rough treatment could the rubber ring take? It was not built to be used in this way, with heavy bodies pulling it in all directions. Just one small tear and we would lose our main flotation. We would still have our individual lifejackets, but our capacity to survive would undoubtedly be further reduced.

As we lifted to the bigger swells, we could sometimes get a quick glimpse of the shoreline. Was it nearer? Perhaps, but in the rough and tumble of the breaking surf how could you be sure? *Don't think about it! Just hang on! Hang on to this ring! Keep your arm under Vicki's shoulder! Hang on! Just hang on!*

The cold and the constant, choking immersion as the waves broke over us chipped insidiously away at the strength of our bodies and at the fabric of our will. It was harder to talk, harder to keep up the front of jollity that held despair at bay. Hopelessness once more hovered at the dark edges. It was so cold. So cold. It would be so easy to slip off into the embrace of mother sea...*Don't think about it! Hang on!* On we drifted, wills and bodies slowly fading in the icy grip of our resignation. So cold. So cold. Why fight? Why bother?

And then, through the insistent rush of wind and water that blocked our ears, came the wavering sound of a lone voice, singing. It was a voice I somehow knew, and the song too felt like an old friend. A lone voice, singing. A lone voice, singing through the storm. A tiny voice, but it could as well have been the massed choirs of the Symphony of a Thousand! Caruso himself could never have sounded sweeter! The bosun Springer, as ever the driving life force, had started up with a faint sea shanty, a lone voice raised hesitantly against the elements that would devour us. A second voice joined in and one by one we took up the refrain. The idea took hold until we had a full-blown chorus singing its defiance through the waves. It was just what we needed to restore our spirits. Sing! Sing! Breathe deep and yell! Ah, the joy of it! Music! Humanity! Hope! On we kept with our impromptu concert for Neptune. We by then had a wealth of repertoire. We could sing for hours! Round and round went the refrains. *In South Australia I was born! Heave away! Haul away! South Australia round Cape Horn! Bound for South Australia!* No longer bound together in the imminence of death, we asserted our unity in life. *Heave away! Haul away!* C'mon lads, we can do it! *Heave away! Haul away!* The louder we sang the better we felt. We would not be beaten! *HEEEAVE AWAAAY! HAAAUL AWAAAY!* God it felt good! All the fear and suffering of the last week combined in one great plaintive life-asserting cry to the deaf heavens. *HEEEAVE AWAAAY!!! HAAAUL AWAAAY!!! HEAAAVE AWAAAY!!! HAAAUL AWAAAY!!!*

Suddenly, unbelievably, the shore was right there, a few hundred yards downwind. We could make out eight or ten figures on the beach. They were looking our way. They had obviously seen us, or maybe heard our crazed refrain borne on the gale. Nearer we came, pushed in bit by bit on each breaking comber. As the bottom shoaled the breakers got steeper and rougher, tumbling us over and over, but we no longer cared. They were pushing us inexorably towards the approaching shoreline. Then – joy! My toes felt the scrape of sand under-foot. New Zealand! There, under my bare soles! We could now pull ourselves and the rubber ring shorewards through the surf, straining against the backwash. The figures on the beach were wading out to meet us. A massive Maori, water up to his chest, pushed on through the waves, his right arm held up, brandishing a bottle of rum. He thrust it into my hands. I drank and passed on the bottle. More guys arrived to help us through the last few remaining yards of surf. Out of the waves I came, the water thigh-high, then knee-high, then ankle-high and finally, gone. Dry land! I threw myself on the beach, spent, shivering with cold and exhaustion, but still burning red-hot inside with the fire of life that, this time at least, had not been extinguished.

13

Out the way! Make room! yelled the bosun's mate, Dave Salt, as he climbed stark naked over the side of the bath. There were already two of us in it. We crowded together in the hot water, throwing it over our frozen bodies, ecstatic at the feel of the warmth thawing our numb extremities. *Aaaah!* was now our sole refrain as we closed our eyes and relished the tingling of returning senses. Encrusted layers of salt from hair, skin and every bodily crevice dissolved into the steaming water, leaving us pink, raw, clean and contented. *For God's sake hurry up, you guys!* There was a queue for the bath. Reluctantly we hauled ourselves from the hypnotic heat of the water and furiously rubbed ourselves down with fresh towels left there for us.

We were in a remote farmhouse, where we had been quickly ferried in the Land Rover. For the placid farmer and his wife it was an invasion from Mars as fourteen hairy, wild-eyed, mildly hysterical ship-wrecked sailors suddenly crowded into their neat little house, dripping water, throwing off rank and sodden clothing, jostling and yelling delightedly with the joy and relief of still being alive, of still being, after all, *here.*

From the farmhouse we were whisked away once more, this time to hospital, for check-ups and observation. It was a tiny hospital at Kaitaia, New Zealand's northernmost town.

It turned out we were big news and we sat and circulated in hospital pyjamas and stripey bathrobes, interviewed by a succession of reporters and policemen and doctors and New Zealand marine department officials. This was all very well, but beneath the brouhaha one question preoccupied us. The ship? How was the ship? Was she salvageable? Could she yet be saved? It was frustrating to be so cared for and cosseted, but at the same time so helpless. If anything could be done to save the *Endeavour II*, it would have to be done quickly. Every inactive hour that passed made any chance of somehow resurrecting the ship less likely. Our question to the constant visitors was always the same. How is the ship? Any news of the ship? The answer was usually an evasive, tight-lipped shrug.

Two long days after coming ashore we were at last taken back to the scene, with no idea of what we would find. We were driven once more over miles of farm tracks, then through the dunes and onto the long sand spit that runs up the southern side of Parengarenga Harbour. As we came down onto the beach itself our apprehension grew. Our last sight of the ship had been of her canted over on the sand bar several miles out to sea, her hull opened up but the great spars still intact. How was she now?

There once more was the sea, flat calm under a grey sky. The storm had wreaked its damage and passed on. We drove north along the sands, searching the flat horizon for a sign – a mainmast still standing perhaps, the dark mass of the hull lying gamely on the bar. Seawards there was nothing. The horizon and all the sea up to it ran clean and unbroken to the distant cliffs to the north. No scar or blemish marred the pristine surface. It was a puzzle. Where on earth the ship? How could two hundred tons of massive timbers be spirited away so completely? On we drove, back to the spot where we had struggled out of the surf. At last we saw some signs that something, some event, had at least happened hereabouts – an increasing litter of broken timbers was scattered along the sand. The mini-bus stopped and we climbed out. The gentlest of breezes ruffled the softly pulsating surface of the sea, which now lapped inoffensively at the shore.

We stood in silence and took in the full measure of the scene that greeted us. There was indeed a hull. There was indeed a mainmast, and a foremast, and a mizzenmast. There were indeed two hundred tons of heavy timbers. They were there all right. Right there under our stunned noses. They covered half a mile of the main beach. They were predominantly in little pieces that you could just about pick up and put into sacks. A semblance of a hull was there, lying on its port side and half-buried in the sand. The masts were there, or sections of them at least, still attached to the hull but ranged around at contorted angles like some wild modernistic sculpture. It was a scene of clinical destruction.

Within a half second the truth was clear – the ship was finished; comprehensively annihilated. The ship was gone. That lovely mahogany hull, once so sleek, once so lively as it pranced through the waves, now lay in its final grave, buried and broken. The artful logic of the masts and rigging had been transformed into a twisted parody of itself, a meaningless bird's nest of tortured inter-weavings. The form, the beauty, the whole principle of the sailing vessel had been ruthlessly deconstructed, piece by piece, leaving an inert and lifeless scrap heap of assorted and unconnected materials. We stared, devastated too, uncomprehending. Nothing, not even the power of the waves that had broken over our cowering backs, could have led us to anticipate such a scene. Our lovely ship was gone. Our dreams were gone. Only our weak flesh, for the moment sickened by these irrevocable losses, clung on, diminished but intact.

A billowing press of sail under furled royals.

I watch from the helm as the spanker is set.

Two hands for the ship as the main course is furled.

The bosun's mate climbs the foremast.

Endeavour II *at anchor off Lord Howe Island.*

The mate (left) and bosun rig a new foretopmast stay, with the cliffs of northern New Zealand in the background.

Heavy weather off the north of New Zealand.

The wreck of the Endeavour II *– 'A semblance of a hull lay half-buried in the sand.'*

'..like some wild modernistic sculpture.'

'..a scene of clinical destruction.'

PART TWO

CAPSIZE

All fear has gone. It was there, as bad as I have known it, but now it has gone. I have crossed some inner boundary, forced a way through the debilitating thickets of bodily concern and found, right here in the maelstrom of wind and water that assaults me, a calm and joy of an intensity never experienced. I am deliriously happy. Every breaking comber that sweeps little Roc from astern, trying to wrest me from my precarious perch on the after-deck, has me laughing out loud. I marvel at the madcap speed of the low clouds streaming pell-mell across a blue but haze-ridden sky. I turn my face astern, closing my eyes in some perverse ecstasy as the gale lashes my cheeks full on. At the top of each crest I revel in the sweep of my momentary kingdom, mile after mile of angry foam-streaked greybeards tumbling after each other in a demonic witches' dance. I do not know if this storm is survivable, but right at this moment I really do not care. I feel I have arrived at some place, some thing, which has taunted and tempted me for years. It is the homecoming of the lost child. I have chanced upon the magnetic centre that has drawn me relentlessly over the horizons. I have entered the beating heart of

*nature itself; implacable, cold, unstoppable, infinitely empow-
ered. I am staring into the unpitying eyes of a steely and
awful truth: that, ultimately, it really doesn't matter.
Nothing really matters. I am subsumed into the wildness
around me, liberated from all concern, freed to scream and
laugh at the naked strength and awful magnificence that
engulfs me. I will never be the same again.*

1

The voyage on *Endeavour II* very nearly killed me, and I could have been forgiven for never wanting to go to sea again. Certainly for the first few months in New Zealand I scarcely thought about once more getting afloat. It was a hectic time. The crew of the *Endeavour II* was very much in the public eye. We were adopted by Auckland's pirate radio station – Radio Hauraki. Over the airways they organised a fleet of cars to come up north, once we were ready to leave hospital, and bring us down to Auckland. They organised their listeners to provide billets for us. They even cajoled Auckland employers to provide temporary jobs. I was lodged with a kind and friendly Auckland couple, Ken and Carol White. I was given a job sweeping a warehouse. It brought in some much-needed money. I had arrived in the country with nothing but the few clothes I was wearing when we were wrecked – a pair of shorts, tee-shirt, oilskin, sou'wester, belt, rigging knife. Not a lot. A great pile of second-hand clothes had arrived at the hospital in Kaitaia, allowing us each to put together a basic ill-fitting wardrobe. I scored an old New Zealand fireman's jacket that I wore for some years after.

I was keen to see as much of the country as soon as possible, so set off with Vicki Watts for a whistle-stop hitch-hike to Bluff, as far south as one can go on the South Island, and back to Auckland. However I needed a decent-paying job to get together some funds for whatever I was going to do next. At that stage I wasn't sure what that was. I had vague ideas about going north to Hong Kong or Japan, but nothing definite. I decided to apply for a job teaching. That would at least pay me professional rates, and give me some spare time too. I got hold of an Education Gazette, and applied for half a dozen jobs around the country. I had no idea where most of the schools were, but decided that I would simply accept the first job I was offered, wherever it may turn out to be.

That was how I came to be a teacher at Hamilton Boys' High School. I had learned from my Tasmanian experience, and had applied for jobs teaching English only. Hamilton is a fairly wealthy city in the heart of New Zealand's main dairy-products region, the Waikato. The school was big, prestigious and run on traditional lines. It had a number of boarders from remoter rural areas, and at first I was lodged in their hostel. For a while after that I shared a house with two other teachers, a classics teacher who wrestled with the composition of knotty poetry, and an American physical education teacher who just wrestled. I then moved out of town to share a farm cottage with another teaching colleague and his wife. This move turned out to be quite significant. For the first few months I concentrated on my job and trying to save some money.

Then two things happened. Firstly I began to realise that New Zealand could be the perfect place to actually build a boat. It was a DIY paradise, with yachting probably only second to rugby as the national obsession. Secondly my pay suddenly shot up. There had been a big pay award for teachers at the same moment as my higher degree from the UK was recognised as meriting a higher pay scale. My salary doubled almost overnight. A plan started to take shape somewhere deep in my mind.

At the same time I had also been quietly processing all that I had learned from the *Endeavour II* debacle. Bit by bit my unforced sub-conscious analysis was surfacing into properly formulated ideas on how, were I to go to sea again, I would want to do it. The basic tenets had taken a definite form within a few months of being washed up on that remote New Zealand shore.

Firstly it had been shown to me that size itself is no guarantee of safety or survival at sea. In fact it was clear that the more extreme the forces acting on a large vessel are, the harder it is for a crew of mere flesh and blood to contain and control those forces. In one sense the *Endeavour II* should never have been lost. By a miracle she had been carried over a shallow bar and been brought up to anchor in sheltered deeper water. The tide eventually carried her back onto the bar, but this was with a mighty *onshore* wind blowing.

It seems inconceivable, from the comfort of the armchair, that some manoeuvre was not tried to either get her sailing again, downwind, against the tide and into the safety of Parengarenga Harbour, or at the very least to have got her sailing adequately enough to have beached her on one of the relatively calm shores of the wide channel in which she was anchored. I have been asked many times why this wasn't done, or at least attempted. I find it next to impossible to answer. The only real answer is *you'd have to have been there to understand why.* The forces acting on the ship were of such power and ferocity that effective management of the ship was more or less ruled out.

I was not privy to the discussions of the officers, but I can quite understand their reluctance to cut the anchor cables. The anchors were the one thing slowing our progress back on to the bar. Any miscalculation, any unforeseen problem with the necessary sailing manoeuvres – both almost certainties under those conditions, would have seen us carried onto the bar in minutes rather than hours. The fact was, the size of the ship meant that it was by then beyond our control. The corollary of this is that the smaller the sailing vessel, the less the risk of it getting beyond control in extreme conditions. From here on, easy unstressful manageability would be an absolute prerequisite for any sea-going vessel.

More important than that, I decided that I would never again put responsibility for my fate in someone else's hands. The decision to weather North Cape in a building north-easterly gale was, to put it mildly, a debatable act of seamanship. I had no control or influence over that decision, and nearly drowned because of it. The conclusion was crystal clear – in future I would only ever go to sea as skipper of my own yacht. If I myself made poor decisions and perished because of them – fine. That I could happily accept. Conversely, I decided also that I would never want the responsibility of someone else's fate on *my* hands. I would never want to be in a position where my own decision-making could lead to someone else's death. Henceforth I would therefore only venture to sea alone, with absolute and total responsibility for myself, nothing more and nothing less.

Purifying the essence of future sea-going down to its most concentrated distillate involved one more pre-requisite – I would have to build my own vessel. Again, for the simple reason of total personal responsibility. Structural failure on *Endeavour II* was by no means the cause of her loss, but we were severely hampered in our ability to get the best out of the ship by the effective decommissioning of the foremast. Under other circumstances that may well have caused the loss of the ship. But the general lesson for me was again quite clear – the strength and seaworthiness of the vessel would have to be down to me and no-one else. I would never again be prey to someone else's poor design or shoddy workmanship.

By building my own yacht I would also know exactly how she was put together. I would be in a far better position to sort out any structural problems, should they arise at sea. As it turned out, it was my intimate knowledge of the construction of the steering system that enabled me to effect a difficult repair at sea, and complete my next voyage successfully. These various threads of argument lead to a simple and inevitable conclusion: if I were to go to sea again, it would be single-handed, in a small and easily managed self-built yacht. The die was cast.

2

By then I had the farm cottage I was renting to myself. My colleague and his wife had bought a house and moved out. The farm itself, ten miles outside Hamilton, was about a hundred and ten acres of prize flat farmland, used mainly for fattening cattle and sheep. I was already getting on well with the farmer, Don Gaskell. He was in his late forties with a wife and three daughters. He appreciated a bit of male company from time to time. Despite the difference in our ages we became great friends. Not far from my cottage was a big unused hay barn. I put the question to Don – how would he feel about letting me use it to build a boat in? He himself was a keen boater – what Kiwi isn't – and was delighted with the idea. *Sure, no problem. Go ahead. I'll help you seal the barn up to make a better workplace.*

Meanwhile I was thinking too about designs and materials. At the time there was a vogue in New Zealand for building ferro-cement boats. Although labour-intensive, it was a cheap method for an amateur, and, if done properly, could produce a very strong hull. I was drawn to the ferro-cement designs of the New Zealand yacht designer Brian Donovan. In the main he designed strong and voluptuously-lined cruising yachts. Time and again I kept coming back to his little gem – his nineteen-foot Nulgarra design.

This was an extraordinarily clever and good-looking set

of lines. On nineteen feet overall he had created a roomy, heavy displacement yacht with almost full headroom, three good berths, galley, room for a useful chart table, a graceful sheer, pretty transom, and with such a well-proportioned coach-roof that from a distance one could mistake the yacht for a twenty-five footer. She was a Bermudan sloop with a good-sized genoa. After much reflection I finally decided that this was the one, and bought the plans.

Thus began almost three years of very hard and very satisfying spare-time work. To loft her lines I bought a wide roll of a thick grey paper used for carpet underlay. This I laid down on the cleared floor of my classroom one weekend, and drew her out. I had bought a beaten up old long wheel-base van for carrying materials, so was all ready to go. I joined the Waikato Ferro-Cement Boatbuilders' Association – a self-help club with a wealth of technical knowledge and a pool of useful equipment. For several years I edited their newsletter, which kept me right up to date with technical developments.

The wire armature for the hull was formed over temporary softwood frames suspended from the roof of the shed. The armature was of high tensile steel rods running longitudinally and diagonally at very close centres, with two layers of half-inch wire mesh on each side. Wire ties to pull the armature together had to be made at every intersection of the rods – literally thousands of them. This took many months of fiddley, hard and very boring work. But I could see a good-looking hull taking shape – even though it was still full of holes...

Finally the hull was ready for plastering – a job done by a team of professionals always used by the club, and therefore very experienced. This is important. Special plaster, with various retarding and plasticising agents, is used. The finished hull has to be as thin as possible – in this case half an inch, but the plaster must cover the armature properly so that it is not exposed to seawater. At the same time it has to be perfectly faired. The hull was first plastered from the outside. It was then left to cure for six weeks or so, draped with sacking, and with an automatic spray system to keep it permanently damp. The team then came back to apply the finishing coat from the inside. Again this was cured for six weeks. The frames could then be stripped out, and there it was! A chunky and immensely strong nineteen-foot hull, just half an inch thick.

I was pleased when the hull-building phase was finished. Neither steel nor plaster are, to me anyway, particularly endearing materials to work with. But that was all behind me. I could now turn to what I always love doing – woodwork. I laminated the deck beams from alternate strips of kauri and Sapele mahogany. Kauri is that wonderful honey-coloured, close-grained New Zealand native pine used so much in yacht construction there. I don't know of any better species of wood to work – it cuts, chisels and planes effortlessly, yet is strong and durable. The deck beams were covered with half-inch marine ply, and a thin kauri-planked deck laid over this.

All the while I was working away on *Roc*, as she was eventually to be named, I made sure to keep in the forefront of my mind the vivid recollections of the *Endeavour II* pounding herself to destruction on the Parengarenga bar. I constantly recalled the sickening sight of the broken ship brought up on the main beach, her massive beams shattered, her planking ripped to matchwood. I wanted to remind myself constantly of the power of the sea, of its limitless destructive force. I was going to go to sea again in a tiny nineteen-foot yacht, but I had no illusions whatsoever about the potential dangers. This time I was going to do it totally on my own terms, with uncompromising preparation.

The Brian Donovan design was already strong, but I increased the scantlings and specifications throughout. In the hull itself I used high tensile in place of mild steel. The rods were more closely spaced. All beams were laminated, not sawn. The deck was twice as thick. The coach-roof itself was built on massive carlins and corner-posts, everything through-bolted. Port-lights were of armoured half-inch glass. I made all the chain-plates and deck fittings – stanchions, pulpit, push-pit, bow roller, Samson post, mast tabernacle – myself, using Don's three-phase welder. They were all oversized mild steel, double hot-dip galvanised. All the standing rigging was increased one size up. I fitted twin forestays and twin back-stays. I have many times heard yachts described as 'overbuilt'. I don't know what that means!

The little yacht had no cockpit well. I wanted to maximise the integrity of the structure, and give myself space and access aft below decks. Nor did I use washboards. The after end of the coach-roof was solid one and a quarter-inch mahogany, through-bolted to the deck beam. I built the cabin roof of half-inch tongue and groove kauri, overlaid with quarter-inch mahogany marine ply. The extreme compound curvature of the shapely small yacht made all the joinery quite difficult, but the end result was a very high strength-to-weight ratio. I really did feel that I could take a sledgehammer to the coach roof and have trouble destroying it. This, as it turned out, was just as well.

The one element of the construction that I would not repeat, were I doing it again now, is the sliding main hatch. I can't remember ever considering an alternative. I just did it. Yachts always have sliding hatches so that's what you do. Certainly a lot of thought went into the baffles, to minimise water ingress, but I don't think I ever thought of using a proper watertight hatch. I now think sliding hatches, however well baffled, are fundamentally unseaworthy, and would never go to sea in a small yacht that had one.

The other element that I now consider a necessary pre-requisite for small-boat ocean sailing, but which I don't think ever crossed my mind at that time, is unsinkability. In these days of high volume, light displacement yachts, and modern closed-cell foams, I really do not understand why so few are designed to be unsinkable. It seems to me it would be relatively easy to design in the required flotation without too much impact on the interior accommodation.

Having now made ocean passages in boats that can sink, and boats that can't, I can attest to the incredible reduction in overall anxiety levels that the latter can produce, particularly in heavy weather. The rigid mother ship, even if awash, is, in my view, a much superior lifeboat to a rubber life-raft. The unsinkable yacht therefore does not need the expense, weight and stowage space for a life-raft. However, even if I had thought about flotation for *Roc*, I doubt it would have been practicable. She was a very heavy boat for her waterline length, and the hundred or so cubic feet of foam needed to keep her afloat would not have left much room inside.

3

Roc gradually took shape. A ton of scrap lead that I had been collecting was melted down into ingots and grouted into the wide keel. The interior was fitted out, pulpit and stanchions bolted on, and the hull sealed with epoxy and painted. Heavy chain-plates were bolted on, and the mast tabernacle fitted. I built a servo-pendulum self-steering gear from timber, plywood and dinghy fittings, to a design by Bill Belcher, the English yachtsman whom I was soon to get to know. The hollow spruce mast and the sails were the only parts made professionally.

My plans too were developing. My general idea was to start heading back towards Europe, via Australia and the India Ocean to Suez and the Mediterranean. However, nothing was definite – I would just see how things went. A few months before the anticipated launch date I realised that the first leg of my proposed voyage – back across the Tasman Sea to Australia – was likely to coincide with the second Single-handed TransTasman Yacht Race, due to start in April 1974. This race, the first of which had been sailed in 1970, was modelled on the early Observer Single-handed Transatlantic Races, which had been sailed every four years since 1960. The course was from New Plymouth, appropriately enough, on the west coast of the North Island, to Mooloolaba, just north of Brisbane on the Queensland coast. The direct distance was about thirteen hundred miles, similar to a Plymouth – Azores voyage.

This was not a crossing to be taken lightly. New Plymouth lies almost in forty degrees south, due east of the Bass Strait. It is therefore very much an upwind course, starting virtually in the Roaring Forties. The Tasman Sea has a justifiable reputation as a very nasty piece of water. Were *Roc* to make a successful crossing, she would be the smallest craft to have done so. In Auckland Harbour, in 1973, I had met and chatted with the amazing sailor John Riding, who had sailed his twelve-foot ocean cruising yacht *Sea Egg* from Europe, via Panama and the Pacific. He was just about to set off across the Tasman to Australia. Sadly he was never heard of again.

I was painfully aware of this, but nevertheless had faith in the uncompromisingly robust construction of *Roc.* I decided that to attempt the crossing as part of the single-handed race would be both an interesting and sociable way of doing it. Quite obviously *Roc* would not be competitive from a racing perspective, but in those days that didn't matter a jot. We knew we were not competing against each other. Our adversary was the ocean. To arrive was, essentially, to win.

So I entered *Roc* for the race. There were, needless to say, in those carefree pre-nanny days, very few rules and conditions. There were no upper or lower limits on yacht size. Skippers had to submit the log of a minimum five hundred nautical mile non-stop voyage in the craft they were entering. Each boat would be subject to a rigorous inspection, out of the water, prior to the race. The organisers reserved the right to refuse entry if they thought the skipper or yacht was for some reason not up to scratch. That was about it.

Roc was still in her shed, in the final stages of construction, when I submitted my entry. A few weeks later a couple of committee members – the chairman Wyn Williams and ex-chairman Howard Vosper – drove up from New Plymouth to have a look at *Roc*. No doubt they wanted to check her out and nip my entry in the bud unless they were totally convinced of her potential seaworthiness. I regaled them for several hours on the finer points of her construction and the thinking behind it. They left seemingly satisfied. As long as my five hundred mile log was satisfactory, and *Roc* passed her final inspection, there would be no objection to her sailing.

At long last, after several thousand hours of labour, *Roc* was fitted into the club steel cradle and, using a tractor to pull her and logs to roll the cradle on, hauled out of the shed into the open air. For the first time I could stand back at a distance and appraise the nearly finished article. I was delighted. Despite her diminutive size, she was without doubt a 'proper' yacht, with her fine proportions, graceful sheer, wide side decks and gleaming bright-work.

The head of art at my school, Les Cook, had designed and painted on the lettering for the yacht's name on the curvaceous transom. The roc was of course the mythical bird that carried Sinbad the Sailor out of his cliff-bound prison, but ROC also, as the perceptive reader will no doubt have already deduced, stood for Roger's Ocean Cruiser. I could now raise the mast and temporarily rig the boat. This period coincided with the end of the school year in December 1973. I resigned from my post after nearly three years at the school. At last I could concentrate full-time on finishing *Roc* and getting her to the start line for the Tasman crossing.

Early one clear sunny morning in January an articulated low-loader reversed into the paddock in front of the shed. *Roc* was jacked up on her cradle, with a crowd of onlookers and willing helpers gathered for the occasion, then lowered on to the truck that was to take her to Auckland. I drove ahead of the truck in my old van. It was a nerve-wracking drive. My pride and joy had left the safety of her shed, but was not yet settled in her proper medium. I was terrified of some mishap on the journey to the sea. We stopped often to check the lashings. The truck drivers, for whom this was just another dull delivery, were impatient with my slow driving, but I refused to speed up.

At last we pulled into Westhaven Yacht Harbour, almost in the shadow of the Auckland Harbour Bridge. A good crowd had gathered, for *Roc* was to be christened and launched immediately. Prominent among the company was Chris Scott, mate of the *Endeavour II*. Chris had been living and working in Auckland since the loss of the ship. Over the previous three years he had often come down to check on *Roc's* progress, his car always loaded with a crate of two of DB Bitter. Many a night he had roped me into some serious Australian-style boozing sessions, ending, if I was lucky, by breakfast time. We were now good cobbers, his initial animosity towards me long forgotten.

There are few things as scary and as magical as seeing a boat you have built slide into the water for the first time. It is scary because at last you will have the answer to the questions that have been tormenting you for months and months. Will she float to her marks? Has the designer got it right? Have *I* got it right? Am I about to have a very public and very embarrassing disaster? Margaret Gaskell, Don's wife, had successfully broken the bubbly and pronounced the immortal words of christening, before *Roc* had rolled slowly into the water on her launching cradle. Aboard were myself and Bob Roberts, one of the leading lights in the boat-builders' club, and a fount of technical knowledge.

As *Roc* floated free from her cradle the magical aspect of a first launching gripped me. *She moves! She is now alive!* It was extraordinary to feel the boat rocking gently for the first time, after years of leaden immobility, to realise that this now really was an actual yacht, a whole entity, no longer just an assemblage of hundreds of painstakingly made parts.

But as I was aboard, I still couldn't answer the scary questions. I couldn't really see how she was floating, and every time I leaned over the side to try and gauge where she was in relation to her marks, I heeled the boat and negated the attempt. I couldn't stand the suspense any longer. *How's she floating, Chris?* I yelled to Chris Scott, who was holding one of her lines ashore. *Good, mate!* came the reply. *You sure? Yeah, she'll be right, no worries.* I still wasn't satisfied. *You absolutely sure? Yeah, mate. You've got pretty much all your boot-topping showing. Don't worry about it.* Roc had been launched in almost full cruising trim, with her mast aboard but not yet raised. I started to relax.

Within half an hour of launching, we had the mast stepped and *Roc* snug in her Westhaven four-pile berth. Almost exactly three years after the loss of the *Endeavour II* I was afloat again. This time I was builder, owner, skipper and crew. My little ship had no engine and no electrical equipment of any sort. I would soon be going to sea again, the personal challenge distilled to as pure and simple a form as it was possible to make it.

4

*'We hereby certify that at 0600 hours on the morning
of 20th March, 1974, Roger Taylor, solo aboard the
yacht* Roc, *did depart Whangarei Heads bound non-
stop for Port Taranaki. Signed R.J.Roberts, Skipper,
yacht* Kopu *and Mr E.Hay, Skipper, yacht* Wakaya,
Whangerei'.

It was the start of my five hundred mile qualifying cruise,
that would take me round the top of the North Island of
New Zealand, scene of so many still-vivid memories, and
down the west coast to Port Taranaki, the large man-made
harbour that served New Plymouth.

Roc had now been afloat and undergoing sea trials,
mainly in Auckland's Hauraki Gulf, for seven or eight
weeks. She was a tough little performer, by no means fast,
but comfortable and reassuring in a seaway. With her
working jib and genoa permanently hanked on to their
respective fore-stays, and the mainsail reefed by a roller
reefing gear that could be operated from the main hatch, she
was easy and simple to sail. The headsails were small
enough that no winches were needed. The self-steering gear
always worked well in a fresh breeze, or with the wind forward of the beam, but was less dependable in light airs with
a following wind. There was no remote adjustment for the

self-steering, so every course change meant a trip aft on deck.

Below she was voluminous for a yacht just fourteen feet on the waterline. There were V-berths forward, with capacious stowage under them. Centrally there was my bunk to starboard, with the galley – a gimballed single burner gas stove with drawers underneath, and a sink unit rescued from a defunct caravan – to port. The aft compartment, under the fully-decked cockpit area, had to starboard a large chart table with navigational stowage under it, and to port my main water tank and more stowage space. The after bulkhead had a hole in it big enough for me to crawl through into the lazaret, where the rudder shaft came through from hull to deck. I had fitted the shaft with an internal tiller, so that *Roc* could, in extreme circumstances, be steered from inside. The fitting of this second tiller was eventually instrumental in the success of my next Tasman adventure, but not at all in the way envisaged.

Bob Roberts, the stalwart of the boatbuilders' club, sailing his self-built forty-footer *Kopu,* decided to accompany me on the first leg of my voyage, from Auckland to Whangarei Heads, about eighty miles up the coast. From there I would set off alone to New Plymouth. We were an unequal partnership cruising north together – little and large, the hare and the tortoise. Bob was very gentlemanly about it, but I developed then and there a dislike of cruising in company that has lasted to this day. The weather alternated between squalls and calms as we made our way up the beautiful coastline with its succession of fine anchorages – Islington Bay on Rangitoto Island, Mansion House Bay on the inshore side of Kawau Island and finally Calliope Bay, a shallow anchorage under the lee of Bream Head, the most easterly headland at Whangarei Heads.

That night a well-heralded storm descended, accompanied by thirty knot winds from the south-east. At four in the morning, as the squalls screamed in, *Roc* began to drag her anchor, bearing down on shoal waters. I laid out my kedge, which fortunately held her. At daybreak, with the assistance of a local skipper, Ted Hayes, aboard his cutter *Wakaya*, I picked up a Northland Harbour Board mooring. This held us snug for the remaining two days of the storm.

By 20th March the wind, although still blowing twenty-five to thirty knots, had veered to south-south-west, now an offshore breeze. At six that morning I weighed anchor and began the beat out through Whangarei Heads. By nine o'clock we had cleared Bream Head and turned north-west to run up the hilly coast, helped on by a fine breeze aft of the port beam. With the genoa poled out and two rolls in the mainsail we sped north, leaving the Poor Knight Islands to starboard. By early evening Cape Brett was astern and we were crossing the wide mouth of the Bay of Islands. Little did I know that one day soon these would become my home waters for four years. Overnight and all the following day the wind eased and veered slowly round to north-west, forcing us further and further offshore.

That day, in ideal sunny and calm conditions, I took and worked my first morning and meridian celestial sights at sea, out of sight of land. For my New Zealand yachtmaster's ticket I had been taught a system using the very compact Martelli's tables. My sextant was a plastic Ebbco – very light and therefore ideal for a small yacht, where in adverse conditions it can often take many minutes to get a good horizon. A reasonably accurate wristwatch, that had been carefully checked and rated by an Auckland watchmaker, was kept below, unworn, as my deck watch, and checked daily against whatever time signals I could pick up on my Sony transistor radio. The system was rudimentary, but it almost always worked well, and got me across six thousand miles of ocean with no navigational mishaps.

All the next day we were virtually becalmed to the north-east of North Cape, visible only at night by the loom of its light. North Cape. I really did not want to go near it. I had seen enough of that stretch of water between the mainland and the Three Kings Islands. I intended to pass to the north of the Three Kings, in deeper, less turbulent water. However the wind continued to veer to east-north-east, freshening all the while. The passage through to Cape Reinga, out of the Pacific Ocean and back to the Tasman Sea, was now a dead run. It was too tempting to pass up.

On the morning of the third day out from Whangarei Heads I squared *Roc* off before the twenty-five knot north-easterly, with just the working jib set, and with some trepidation started the run through between the mainland and Three Kings Islands. It was a wild ride in the inevitable steep seas, but *Roc* ran on comfortably, rising easily to the towering crests overtaking her from astern. As we closed Cape Reinga, the north-west headland of New Zealand, we gybed from port to starboard tack to ease her gently offshore again and avoid the steeply shoaling area off the cape.

By evening we had cleared Cape Reinga and *Roc* had her first look at the Tasman Sea. Her introduction could not have been more appropriate. By midnight the wind had gone round to the east and was up to thirty knots. We were now almost close-hauled under minimal sail, heading south by east along the coast. Although it was an offshore wind the sea was nasty and uncomfortable, with the easterly gale vying with a huge westerly swell to see which could create the most havoc.

All the next day the barometer stayed low, and the easterly gale blew on. At one o'clock the next morning the wind backed to north-east, easing off to twenty-five knots. As morning broke the wind gradually eased further and I shook out the deep reef in the main. We were now making five knots with a beam wind. By afternoon we were bowling along with full main and genoa in a perfect breeze. Had I known what was to come, I might have savoured the moment a little more than I did.

By midday on the seventh day out from Whangarei Heads we had already covered four hundred and ninety miles – a respectable average of seventy miles a day – so were close to achieving the qualifying distance. New Plymouth lay a mere ninety-seven miles to the south. Nearly there.

In fact it took four days to cover those last miles. The wind crept away and refused to come back. During the day-time, as *Roc* lay slatting back and forth in the south-east swell under a clear blue sky, the symmetrical slopes of Mount Egmont, the volcanic peak that dominates the Taranaki peninsula, taunted me to the south-east, seemingly never getting any nearer. At night the loom of bright lights to the south, that I took to be New Plymouth, took over the mocking role. Every night the light show got marginally nearer. I had not realised that New Plymouth was such an evidently big metropolis.

Finally, after three days of immobility, a proper wind came up from the north-east, late in the evening. Ahead was a growing spread of coastal lights. They could only be New Plymouth. And yet...I could not pick up any of the navigational lights. There was something disconcerting about the brightness of the lights and their overall pattern and texture. Something was not right.

As I bore down on them with a good breeze on the port quarter, the groups of lights separated out. They suddenly seemed very close. Were they a mass of little fishing dories fishing by strong lamplight? At one point I thought they were just a few hundred yards in front, but I kept on sailing

and still did not reach them. Then each dazzling light started to divide into a long string of individual lights. They were much further away than I had thought. For three hours I sailed towards the lights, which now spread across the sea in front of me like dozens of huge and brightly lit birthday cakes.

As I finally came close enough to see properly what lay ahead, the reality dawned. What had originally seemed like individual bright lights were the scores of bulbs strung all round the working decks of a sizeable Japanese squid boat. I counted thirty-five of these boats – a huge fishing fleet jagging for squid just outside territorial waters. Cruising amongst them was a massive mother ship. It took me an hour to sail through the fleet.

I had not slept all night and at five in the morning I decided to take a short nap. As always I set my alarm to wake me in thirty minutes. I did not hear it. Luckily I woke, about two hours later, knowing immediately I had overslept. I rushed to the hatch and was horrified to see us bearing down on the shore to the south of New Plymouth. In an hour at the most we would have run onto it. With the freshening breeze the self-steering gear had not held course. We now had a long beat back north, against the tidal stream, to Port Taranaki.

It took until early afternoon to reach the Port Taranaki breakwater, where we were met by a New Plymouth Yacht Club patrol boat that took us to our mooring. We had logged six hundred and sixty-five nautical miles. *Roc* had been fully blooded. She was a plucky little sea boat and I felt confident about the challenge ahead. I knew it would be tough. I was right.

5

By 1974 there had been four transatlantic single-handed races and one trans-Tasman race. The race I was entering was therefore the sixth oceanic single-handed race ever held. This sort of yachting event was in its infancy and was still simple in conception and pure in execution. The distorting clutches of commercialism had not yet managed to get a grip on the sport.

For this race ten skippers, from a range of backgrounds, and with a forty-year age span, turned up one by one with their various, mainly small, yachts, several of them self-built. No skipper had any sponsorship or outside help. We were self-financing and, in every way imaginable, self-sufficient. There were no shore crews apart from the occasional spouse or friend, no back-up teams, no twenty four hour manned communications centres feeding information back and forth, no public relations executives, no garish logos plastered on hulls and sails turning them into floating bill-boards, no corporate promotions, no razzmatazz, no showers of champagne, and, perhaps most importantly, no aspirations on the part of the skippers beyond quietly getting on with the challenge in hand, exercising their best seamanship, and arriving safely at the other end.

I was by then twenty-six years old, and was, by a couple of years, the youngest skipper in the race. The oldest was the other Englishman, Bill Belcher, who had designed my self-steering system. Bill, together with his wife Aileen, had sailed his T24 *Raha* out from England a few years previously. All told, we were a motley collection. There was the one-legged mariner, John Jury. Annette Wilde, one of the first female single-handed skippers, had built her own thirty-three-foot ferro-cement yacht *Valya*. From Australia came the retired Sydney stockbroker Charles Ure, and the veterinary surgeon Ian McBride. John Mansell was Chief Officer on the inter-island ferries, while Pony More was Sailing Master of the sail training ship *Spirit of Adventure*. Joe Davidson, an unassuming New Plymouth warehouseman in his mid forties, entered another self-built yacht, the twenty-two-foot *White Heron*. Finally there was the only multi-hull entrant, the thirty-eight-foot trimaran *Rebel II*, skippered by the young South Islander Tony Allan.

Seven out of the ten yachts entered were less than thirty feet overall. Most of the yachts were at the heavier end of the displacement spectrum. Not one of them could be called an out-and-out ocean racer. There was no marina or facilities for yachts to lie alongside at Port Taranaki, so as the contestants arrived they were assigned to swinging moorings in the harbour. The only opportunity for the public to see the yachts up close was on the day of the hull inspections when, after being lifted out by crane and held in the slings for inspection, we were rafted alongside one of the main ship wharves for the afternoon. There was of course a great deal of interest in the event and we all did several interviews for newspapers and yachting magazines. But it was all low-key. There was no media feeding frenzy, and we were glad of that.

I did suffer one severe embarrassment during the week leading up to the start. I was aboard *Roc* one evening when a small launch drew alongside. With the driver of the launch was a policeman. *You Roger Taylor?* he asked. *Yes, I am.*

How can I help? He looked a bit sheepish. *Well, I'm sorry to have to say this, but you're under arrest.* My brain raced. Good God! What have I done? *What on earth for?* I asked, my head still reeling. It was the Tuesday before the Saturday race start. Arrested! What was going on? Would it mean I couldn't sail on Saturday? *I'm enforcing a court order against you for civil debt. I'm afraid I have to take you into custody until the debt is discharged. I'd appreciate it if you could accompany me now to the police station.*

I closed up *Roc* and boarded the launch. Fifteen minutes later I was locked up in the New Plymouth police cells, banged up, with a hard wooden bed, a thin blanket and a bucket in the corner. I hadn't paid my bill for the insurance premium for the road transport of *Roc* to Auckland a few weeks earlier. I'd never received the bill, had been afloat for most of the intervening period and had, stupidly, forgotten all about it. The Hamilton insurance broker, rather than contacting me in New Plymouth, had applied to the court in Hamilton to have me arrested. Well, it was his right, I suppose, and it was certainly a sure-fire, if rather excessive, strategy for getting his payment.

It was mid-evening when my cell door clanged shut and the key was turned in the lock. I would be held overnight then accompanied to my bank to arrange payment. If that were not successful I would be brought back to my cell and held until payment was made. Simple.

Later that evening a visitor was shown into my cell – Howard Vosper, of the race organising committee. He was a funeral director by profession, so well used to dealing with people who thought the end of the world had come. I was acutely embarrassed, and worried about publicity that might bring the race into disrepute. He was understanding and supportive, and did his best to help me see the funny side of the situation. I felt better for his visit. I spent a restless night in clink.

Next morning I was taken to an interview room to wait for the bailiff who was going to accompany me to the bank. The old wooden table was a mass of carved details of prisoners and their various sins. *WH 5yrs GBH. Smiffy 8 yeers aggrivated robery.* I was tempted to add my own criminal record to the honour board: *R Taylor, one night, civil debt,* but thought better of it. The debt was soon discharged, and so was I.

On my way back to *Roc* a couple of reporters waylaid me at the harbour. They obviously knew what had happened and fired a few tentative questions at me. I wasn't in the mood, and snapped at them that I had nothing to say. To their credit they didn't press the issue and nothing was ever reported.

6

27th April 1974. Port Taranaki. It was a grey, gusty day, with the barometer falling and the weathermen forecasting gales. Just the day to take my tiny yacht out into the Roaring Forties. Ah well. I was committed and that was that. My water tank was full and my stores stowed. Many hands had been shaken and soft cheeks kissed. A great crowd had gathered on the breakwater. HMNZS *Inverell* was anchored in the harbour, dressed for the occasion, starting gun primed. Somewhere amongst the gold braid and extravagant hats on board her was the Official Starter, Dame Annabelle Rankin, the Australian High Commissioner in New Zealand.

At 1045 hours I slipped my mooring under jib and reefed main and joined the other nine yachts jilling for position near the starting line. The five-minute flag went up. There was no turning back now. A great puff of smoke from *Inverell* preceded, fractionally, a good navy-quality bang, and we were off.

The twenty-knot breeze was from the south-east, giving us an almost straight run through the harbour entrance and out to sea. Of that I was glad. We could all get a quick offing, away from the watching eyes, in a fairly tight group. It was inevitable I would soon be left behind by the nine quicker yachts. With a following wind I would keep up for a bit longer. As we pulled away from the land, rising to the purposeful swells, the wind increased and swung slowly round to south-west. One by one I was overhauled by the competing yachts, with a wave and a last shouted *Good luck!* Before long I was on my own. I of course did not know it then, but I would be on my own for the next thirty-five days.

The weather deteriorated rapidly. By two in the afternoon I was putting more rolls in the mainsail as the wind reached twenty-five knots. I had a succession of small disasters that transported me instantly from the comforts of life ashore to the realities of small-boat ocean sailing. Firstly one of the lines from my self-steering gear to the tiller broke. *Roc* inevitably went off course. I hauled myself on deck to unlock the wind vane. I pulled out the locking pin without thinking. The vane spun round violently and the lead counterweight caught me fair on the cheek. Luckily it was just on the fleshy part under my cheekbone. I have no doubt that if it had struck me an inch higher my cheekbone would have been fractured.

The boat was by now out of control as I nursed my cheek, cursing my stupidity. We gybed and the boom cracked me fair and square on the side of the head. I now had two painful bumps to think about, but I needed to get *Roc* back on course. I grabbed some spare line and my well-sharpened rigging knife to cut a new steering line. I cut the line, but in the process almost sliced off the top of my left index finger. Blood everywhere! Hastily I wrapped a handkerchief tightly round my finger to stem the flow. It was soon bright red. Somehow I got the boat settled and went below to attend to all my wounds. Battered, bruised and bleeding I sat on my bunk and fought off the nausea that was welling up inside. Welcome to the Tasman Sea...

The south-easterly gale increased and increased. By late afternoon I had taken in the mainsail completely, and was running to the north-west under jib only. By midnight I was lying under bare poles in forty knots of wind in a rising sea. At six in the morning, still battened down, my log entry said it all:

Seas huge (15'?) and breaking right over ship. Very wet below.

The storm continued without a let up. For my noon position I made the entry:

Don't know and don't care!

I tried setting the tiny storm jib to give us some more speed in the right direction, but even that was too much for the conditions.

At five that afternoon, just thirty hours out from New Plymouth, disaster struck. A big sea hit *Roc*, carrying her round on to the other tack. I heard an innocuous clunk. I didn't think much about it until I looked on deck through the aft port-light and saw that the tiller was swinging loosely. I crawled through into the lazaret and checked the steering system. The coupling that held the two halves of the rudder shaft together had shattered.

The rudder and the tiller were no longer joined. A stainless steel shaft came up from the rudder. A stainless steel shaft came down from the tiller. Nothing now connected them. Both shafts revolved happily to and fro in their independent gyrations, freed from the stress and strain of having to hold a course. How nice for them, I thought.

My position was now somewhat vulnerable. I had been unable to take any sights in the storm conditions, so could not be sure of my exact position. I had estimated that my drift was about one knot to the north-west, away from the land, but of this I could not be totally sure. What would happen if the wind veered to the west? I would be set towards a lee shore, with no steering. I prepared for an emergency, putting on warm, dry clothing, stowing flares in a sail bag, making sure I had a knife handy to cut my life-raft lashings.

But all I could do was drift, wait and suffer. The gale kept on all that night, easing very slowly. All night and all the next day I was cold, wet and miserable, undecided about what to do. One voice kept arguing to pack it in, to rig some emergency steering, once conditions allowed, and high-tail it back to New Plymouth, back to warmth, safety, hot food, human contact, feminine embraces... The other voice said *Like hell! Sort out the problem and get on with it!*

By five that afternoon the wind was down to twenty-five knots and the seas were coming off the boil. I decided to see if I could somehow reunite the two halves of the rudder shaft. I loaded myself up with tools and squeezed awkwardly into the tiny lazaret. I had an idea in mind, but no certainty that it would work.

First I removed the remaining pieces of the shattered coupling. It was an iron casting, evidently not up to the job. Then I started to explore whether my plan might work. This centred on the emergency tiller fitting which I had put on the shaft, to enable me to steer from inside should I want. This was a solid stainless steel sleeve that fitted over the shaft, kept in place by bosses. I suspected that if I could free this up and move it down the shaft, I may be able to use it as a coupling. It depended on whether all the machined parts were interchangeable, and whether I could physically move and reconnect everything.

Cramped uncomfortably in the bucking confines of the lazaret, I hammered and grunted for several hours. It worked. By nightfall I had the shaft reconnected. However the total job was by no means finished. The reconnection meant that the main tiller was now at ninety degrees to the centreline.

I would have to doctor and rebuild the tiller fitting on deck. I turned in exhausted, but a little happier.

The next day was perhaps the most crucial of this voyage. It would determine whether I could devise a workable steering system again, and whether I would decide to press on across the Tasman, or turn back. At two in the morning, with these questions evidently preoccupying me, I turned out on deck to continue the work. I removed the main tiller and thought about the fundamental alterations I was going to have to make.

The tiller was bolted to two mild steel cheeks welded to the sleeve at the top of the rudder shaft. One of these cheeks would have to be cut off entirely. The other would have to be bent round ninety degrees and the tiller reattached to it. I would then have a weakened, but workable, system.

The wind slowly fell to fifteen knots and backed to the north-east – a perfect beam wind. I worked away all morning, dividing my time between the tiller fitting, cleaning and drying out the ship, and ascertaining my position. To cut through the two-inch by quarter-inch steel tiller cheek I had one blunt hacksaw blade, without the saw. It took several hours of patient and painful work, sawing endlessly back and forth, with the blade cutting my fingers as much as the steel.

The sun was now out, and I was able to take morning and noon sights and establish my position – one hundred and twenty miles from New Plymouth and just south of my track. By one in the afternoon *Roc* was sailing again, reaching comfortably to the north-west at a steady four knots, with a moderate sea and bright sunshine. Everything was now well with the world. My mind was made up. We would carry on. I wrote in my log:

Had to make the big decision – carry on or return?
The jury steering is not the best, but I'm not giving

up. Beautiful fair breeze and one tenth of the trip done – KEEP GOING!! Just making that decision, and getting the ship sailing again in perfect conditions was a great morale booster. Obviously I'm out of any chance for the handicap trophy – but I'll be there!

I wonder now whether I would have been so confident had I known what was in store over the next four days. Our trial by water had hardly begun.

We enjoyed an afternoon and evening of superb sailing in the ideal conditions and for the first time I started to enjoy myself. After midnight the breeze started to freshen and I took a couple of rolls in the mainsail. Shortly after I changed the headsail from genoa to jib. All night the wind continued to increase, and by five in the morning I had lowered the working jib and set the storm jib on the inner fore-stay.

Despite the reduced sail we were plunging comfortably on at a steady four knots. The steering and self-steering were both working well. I was able to stretch out on my bunk and relax with a book. Compared to *Endeavour II*, *Roc* was a quiet vessel at sea. There was none of the constant creaking and groaning of timber frames and planking. The simple rig did not set up a cacophonous wailing in the wind. There was nonetheless a certain amount of squeaking, particularly from the mainsheet blocks.

As I lay there that morning, engrossed in my book, I realised that I could hear what sounded like a ghostly human voice, shouting a distant *Heyyyyy!* I ignored it, dismissing it as the sort of aural illusion commonly experienced by single-handers. It was just the sound of a block working some-where, which my senses were stupidly misinterpreting. I read on, but the cries came more urgently over the wind – *Heyyyy! Heyyyy!*

Finally I had to investigate. I poked my head through

the main hatch and was shocked to find us crossing just a hundreds yard or so behind the stern of a Japanese fishing boat. She was rearing her way to windward, straight into the big seas. A crowd had gathered on her after-deck and was waving and shouting. I waved back. I was uncomfortably aware that we were very close to a collision. We were well away from any shipping lanes but my watch-keeping was, I realised, too slack. I would have to be more careful in future.

By evening it was gusting to thirty-five knots and the seas were looking more ominous. I had already learned from experience that gales from the easterly quarters throw up the worst seas in the eastern Tasman, with its west-bound currents. This was once again being borne out. The wave crests were starting to break and tumble.

Just before eleven that night we were hit by an express train. A wall of water slammed into *Roc* square on the starboard beam with a jarring thud and roar, and carried her over well beyond the horizontal. *Roc* struggled back upright again. Below was a royal mess, with everything strewn indiscriminately around the cabin. Checking on deck I found that the self-steering servo pendulum had jumped out of its pintles and was in danger of being carried away. I secured that, and took down the small amount of sail we were carrying.

By midnight the gale had backed slightly to north-north-east, and was now up to forty knots. We lay-to under bare poles, taking regular sickening thumps on the beam. I slept intermittently, now glad beyond measure that I had built my little ship so strongly. Overbuilt? No such thing.

At first light I looked on deck and was horrified to see the self-steering vane tottering precariously. The top bearing had gone and the vane had fallen, hooking itself over the rope safety line across the counter. Nothing was actually holding it to the ship any more. I grabbed it quickly and lashed it to the deck for the time being. Both the main elements of the self-steering gear had almost gone over the side within the last eight hours. I had been lucky to retrieve them.

The gale started to ease slowly, and by midday was down to thirty knots. That afternoon I was able to go on deck to start repairing the self-steering gear, in readiness for sailing again. However by then I had another major problem to sort out. During the night my flag halyard, a light line to the spreaders, had broken loose and wrapped itself round and round the top section of the mast. There was no way I could set any sail without clearing the mess. To do this I would have to go aloft. The seas were as yet too rough for me to attempt this, but conditions were improving rapidly as the depression moved quickly away.

By four in the afternoon, with the wind down to fifteen knots and the seas much smoother, I knew I had to get on with it. All *Roc's* running rigging was made up of good solid rope, led to a pin-rail around the base of the mast. Bunched all together this gave me a good handful to grip. With my legs around the mast I pulled myself up to the spreaders on the married running rigging. I was able to get a leg over the spreaders and sit there, clinging to the mast with my legs and one arm. With the other arm I slowly freed the tangle of line around the mast. With no sail up we were gyrating around alarmingly, but at that relatively low height, about fifteen feet, it was nothing compared to being aloft on *Endeavour II*. By five we were under way again, but the wind continued to die and at eleven in the evening I dropped all sail to stop it slatting back and forth. We were totally becalmed.

For five hours we went round in circles as the odd zephyr took us one way or the other. I might have enjoyed the respite from the heavy weather we had experienced so far, but I was worried. The barometer was falling rapidly. Despite the clear skies and light winds, we seemed destined for yet more nasty weather.

7

It came up slowly from the south-east. For almost twelve hours under a bright sun, one whole span of daylight, we had a benign following breeze of ten to fifteen knots. We were once more settled in to our usual cruising speed of four knots. At five that afternoon, out of nowhere, a tremendous squall hit us, gybing the mainsail with a terrific crash. Fortunately I had a preventer set. Within less than two hours we were once again running under bare poles in thirty-five knots of wind.

I tried to cook my evening meal, but the gas stove would not light. I had, stupidly in retrospect, fitted a mushroom vent over the stove, on the side deck. Seawater had got through the vent and doused the stove. The solid minerals in the seawater had blocked the tiny jet for the gas. I had no means of unblocking it. No more hot food, no more hot drinks. It was not a pleasant prospect as the gusts came in stronger and stronger. By midnight it was worse than we had seen it so far, well over forty knots. It was hard to believe that once again a violent storm was building, the third within less than a week.

It blew all night, quite relentlessly, a cold Antarctic severe gale from the south-south-east. By dawn the seas had got themselves up to a fine old fury. It was a nasty, lumpy sea, with dangerous cross swells. The crests were reaching higher and higher, breaking forward with a frightening hiss. Lying-to, the tiller lashed to leeward with shock cord, *Roc* took up a position more or less beam on to the advancing combers. I knew she was very vulnerable to another knockdown in this attitude, but my options were limited. I would have liked to steer her downwind from inside. That had been my planned tactic for these conditions. However the inside tiller fittings had been butchered to repair the rudder shaft, so that option was out.

I realised at that point that I had made a mistake in my preparation, by not having on board some proper streaming gear that may have helped her to lie stern-on. Whether it would have made much difference to such a small heavy boat is difficult to say. There was also the potential difficulty and danger of deploying and retrieving warps in survival conditions. I had certainly had doubts about the usefulness and practicality of towing warps from *Roc,* and so had not followed it up during my preparation. Now I regretted the decision. At that moment I would have tried anything within reason that may have helped *Roc* present less lateral area to the hungry combers growling and hissing around her.

It was only a matter of time before *Roc* found herself in the wrong place at the right moment. At about eleven that morning a breaking crest hit us square on, throwing *Roc* once again on to her beam ends. It was, admittedly, not as bad a knockdown as the last one, that had turned her partially upside down, but for the first time on this voyage my nerve started to waver. The sea had now built up to a different order of threat. The storm looked well set, with the barometer unmoving at its lowest reading so far. Outside, ragged low cloud scudded rapidly across the sky. Occasionally an ironic sun shone briefly, grinning through the hazy atmosphere. Below, water dripped everywhere, having forced itself through the sliding hatch as smaller seas broke over us.

I sat disconsolate on my bunk, clinging to the companionway ladder for support. Sometimes a comber broke just fore or aft, with a roaring hiss that died quickly away as the foaming water subsided back to the wave face. If the storm kept up, as it seemed it would, the chances of avoiding yet another knockdown were virtually non-existent.

So far *Roc* had proved herself strong enough for the challenge, but doubts, encouraged by my tiredness after days of heavy weather, were starting to creep in. The hull was, after all, only a half-inch thick. One half of one inch. No more than the width of my little finger!

It suddenly seemed laughable. Could *Roc's* hull really withstand tons of water smashing into it at speed? If we were picked up and dumped into a trough, how on earth could all that painstakingly assembled steel and wire and plaster hold together? If the hull were breached *Roc* would fill in no time. Would I have time to get the life-raft off before she sank below the surface and began her graceful spiral down into the cold depths, lost forever? Would I be trapped inside for *Roc's* final journey to that black unknowable world?

I thought of John Riding, lost in these self-same waters just a few short months before. It would take so little now for me to join him. Our fates were separated by nothing more than that one fragile membrane, no thicker than the width of one tiny finger.

8

I had made myself a jam sandwich for my lunch and was halfway through eating it, still, fortunately, with an arm wrapped round the companionway ladder, when the wave hit us. No... on thinking about it and trying to relive those first few seconds as accurately as memory will allow, it is not enough to say that the wave just hit us. It consumed us. It took us into its great, black, pitiless, roaring maw and swallowed us whole. We were no longer on the water, we were inside it.

It was just after noon, but the world went black as we were carried over and into the throat of the wave. Its watery jaws clamped over us with an ear-shattering roar, reinforced from inside *Roc* as the contents of every drawer and locker emptied and flew willy-nilly around the cabin, crashing and smashing into what was now its lowest point – the coach-roof. In the black spinning mayhem I clung to the ladder, knowing that this was the end. This was not survivable. It felt as if every square inch of the hull was being crushed to powder. I had instinctively closed my eyes, for protection, and was waiting for the final rush of cold water that must surely come, driving us down forever.

The roaring ebbed away and gravity brought me back onto my bunk, where I had been sitting, except that the ply top and cushion were no longer quite there. I opened my eyes. Light came through the port-lights. We were upright again. Icy water sloshed six inches deep on the cabin sole. *Oh God, I knew it, we've been holed.*

I looked round the cabin, now scarcely recognisable. The whole interior of the boat had been rearranged. The ply bunk tops and cushions were spread-eagled at crazy angles. Stores and equipment had been thrown everywhere into a mad jumble. The drawers of the galley had slid out and emptied themselves, catapulting cutlery and cooking utensils in every direction. Worse still, sticky goo was dripping from the cabin ceiling over everything. Broken glass was scattered everywhere. My jars of preserved plums and tomatoes had fallen from their store under the forward bunks and smashed on the cabin top.

I took all this in with disbelief but at that moment it was not my concern. The hull must be damaged. I had to find where as quickly as possible. One advantage of such a small boat is that you can inspect the below-waterline part of the hull pretty quickly. I couldn't find any signs of damage. A belated thought struck me – the mast! Is it still standing? I looked tentatively up through the skylights in the hatch, fearing the worst. The mast was still there, apparently intact. The water level inside the boat was still the same. All this water must have been forced through the sliding hatch baffles by the pressure within the wave. I quickly pumped it out, my mind racing.

We seemed to have come through a total inversion with no apparent damage, but surely, surely, we could not be so fortunate a second time. The unearthly roaring, heard from the inside of the wave, played and replayed itself in my head. I simply could not allow it to happen again. I could not just sit there, my will eroded by fear, and wait passively for the next hammer blow. I had to do something. I just somehow had to grasp some control of the situation. There was no alternative. I would have to go on deck and steer.

I struggled into my harness, slid the hatch forward a little way, and climbed out on to the after deck, closing the hatch behind me. The wrecked cabin I had left behind suddenly seemed warm and safe and inviting, as for the first time I felt the full blast of the storm and glimpsed the awesome seascape stretching away to a hazy horizon.

However my attention was quickly diverted elsewhere. The self-steering gear! The wind vane, a piece of plywood strengthened with aluminium framing, was bent at a crazy angle, the plywood shattered in the middle. I crawled aft on the counter to inspect the rest of the gear. The servo-pendulum, that simple but clever device that created the power to steer the boat, still hung on its pintles. There was just one problem. All that remained was the top two feet or so. The pendulum, laminated from kauri and jarrah, an Australian hardwood, had snapped off at the waterline.

My stomach lurched. *Oh nooo!* I had no ready-made spare, only a baulk of kauri lashed on the side deck. I no longer had a workable self-steering gear. If we were to survive this storm, there was still the best part of a thousand ocean miles to cover. I would have to hand steer all the way.

A wave swept *Roc*, taking me up to my chest in water. The self-steering problem could wait. I settled myself on the flush-decked cockpit, my harness attached to a strong point, and unlashed the tiller. *Roc* slowly responded as I turned her downwind and we began our mad, magical flight before the pursuing breakers.

Flight. Fugue. We settled bit by bit into a rhythm, gradually finding our own harmonious equilibrium in the maelstrom of conflicting forces. Little *Roc*, heavy but buoyant, rose up and up as each huge swell passed underneath, bringing us effortlessly to a hilltop peak. For a few heart-stopping seconds the world lay spread below us, a churning primeval fury as far as the eye could see. Then down, down into the deep trough. The very sky seemed blocked out as the black wave faces rose up around us, overhanging, threatening, doom-laden. Surely they must devour us. But no, the theme, always slightly transposed, repeats itself.

Up we start again, slowly, slowly at first, then gathering pace as the wave face steepens, throwing us once more up into the clouds. The world is still there, the world as we now know it, that is, a wild watery kingdom, alien, merciless, uncaring, monstrously powerful. That is all there now is. My universe is now no more than a tiny makeshift platform, squeezed and oscillating between a raging ocean and a ragged sky. I sit hunched on my few square feet of fragile decking, a glorified tea tray, and ride the roller-coasting combers.

Occasional one catches us, sweeping the deck in a tumble of foamy water. I am often up to my neck in it. I no longer care. I suddenly feel an overwhelming sense of privilege. What a rare and priceless thing it is, to witness this, to be allowed into this elemental scene and for a few precious hours to scratch at the raw edge of life and nature itself. My fear ebbs softly away, replaced by a hot and inexpressible delirium.

Every breaking comber that sweeps little Roc from astern, trying to wrest me from my precarious perch on the after deck, has me laughing out loud. I marvel at the madcap speed of the low clouds, streaming pell-mell across a blue but haze-ridden sky. I turn my face astern, closing my eyes in some perverse ecstasy as the gale lashes my cheeks full on. At the top of each crest I revel in the sweep of my momentary kingdom, mile after mile of angry foam-streaked greybeards, tumbling after each other in a demonic witches' dance. I do not know if this storm is survivable, but right at this moment I really do not care. I feel I have arrived at some place, some thing, which has taunted and tempted me for years. It is the homecoming of the lost child. I have chanced upon the magnetic centre that has drawn me relentlessly over the horizons. I have entered the beating heart of nature itself: implacable, cold, unstoppable, infinitely empowered. I am staring into the unpitying eyes of a steely and awful truth: that, ultimately, it doesn't really matter. Nothing really matters. I am subsumed into the wildness around me, liberated from all concern, freed to scream and laugh at the naked strength and awful magnificence that engulfs me. I will never be the same again. It is my one, glorious moment of epiphany, beyond sanity, translucent, irretrievable.

For three hours I rode the storm on deck, weaving a safe path through the mountainous seas, entranced by the madness of it all. Slowly the imperatives of my body reasserted themselves, dragging me back down from the transcendent plane I had somehow reached. Exposed on the deck, regularly submerged in the icy breakers, I grew colder and colder. I started to shiver, my concentration wavered, and I knew that I could not sustain my position on deck for much longer. I was close to hypothermia. The choice was stark. Stay on deck to keep the boat at a better attitude to the seas, and risk death from exposure, or go below, leaving *Roc* to lie to as she will, and risk another knockdown.

I went below, abandoning *Roc* and myself to our fate. Once more drifting helplessly amongst the hissing combers, my fear returned. I reverted to a dull state of terror. We were back to the norm; the overriding drive to save one's skin, to avoid, at any cost, a confrontation with one's own mortality. My moments of abandon and enlightenment had been a wondrous thing, but now I was sick of this storm, sick of this endless cycle of heavy weather, sick of the days of lying under bare poles, sick of my lack of progress, sick of the unceasing assault on my little yacht. I once more prepared to abandon ship. I could no longer sit or lie on my bunk. I could only stand, head pushing against the coach-roof, hands locked on the grab-rails, moaning to myself as a comfort. I set up a mantra-like chant; *Please ease seas...Please ease seas...Please ease seas...*

My ears were tuned in keenly to the passage of the growling waves around us, but even more so to the rhythm and cadence of the wind in the rigging. It seemed as if the heavy gusts were just a fraction less frequent. Was it my imagination, just wishful thinking, or was the tone of the wind falling slightly? The barometer had pushed up a notch. By nightfall there was no doubt. Conditions were easing. By ten that night the wind had dropped to twenty knots or so. We were no longer threatened by tumbling breakers. Relief flooded through me, into every last cell of my body.

We had been through hell and, literally, high water. Little *Roc* had been picked up and dumped on her head. Below she was an unimaginable mess, but she was still floating, undamaged. The mast, deliberately overbuilt and over-rigged for just this sort of eventuality, had stood up manfully to the enormous strains put on it. Our self-steering gear was damaged beyond repair. That was a terrible set-back for a single-hander, but what the hell, it could have been much worse.

I suddenly realised that today was a Saturday. We had been at sea just over a week. It seemed like an eternity. We were about four hundred miles along our route, almost one third of the way. At midnight the wind dropped right down and swung round to the south-west, a beam wind. I slept for a few hours to regain my strength and at seven went on deck to start the next phase of the voyage. I was delighted to find that with a bit of tweaking I could, in this wind, get *Roc* to sail herself more or less on our desired course. The barometer continued its rise. The wind blew steadily at a benign ten to fifteen knots out of the south-west. *Roc* plunged on under her own steam at her usual four knots. I rested and intermittently tried to impose order on the mayhem below. All was again well with the world.

9

Ah, the sea. Ever changing, always ready with a sudden shift or surprise, reliably unreliable, happy to stroke your head gently before kicking you in the teeth, fickle, moody, endlessly fascinating, endlessly frightening, seductive, bullying, irrepressible, irresponsible, unfathomable, hateful and adorable. After a week of shaking us by the scruff of the neck and roaring angrily that we *should not pass here!* it put on its best toothy grin, bowed obsequiously, bobbed its head, and with a *please...the pleasure's all mine...* waved us magnanimously through...

Day after day we wafted gently on in perfect sailing conditions. For four days the wind kept more or less in the south-west, not too strong, not too light, and *Roc* sailed herself day and night. We were averaging a distance made good of about eighty miles from noon to noon. The little row of crosses extended slowly across the chart. I slept long and well, read, worked my sights and tried to develop a taste for cold tinned food.

We were well into the second week, the one I usually find the worst. This is for me the time when loneliness sets in, a sort of despair at the distance and remoteness from friends and family, a longing, a fear that they may never be seen again. For the first week one is too busy getting into the sea-going routine, by the third week one is settled in to a groove that can continue indefinitely. The second week is the one that hurts. As I wrote simply in my log on Day 12:

Very depressed all day. Lonely.

After four days of relaxed sailing, as *Roc* looked after herself, the wind veered further to the south, onto the port quarter. It was the moment I had been dreading. However much I fiddled with the balance of the ship, it was impossible to persuade *Roc* to hold a steady course. There was nothing for it. I would have to hand steer.

I steered the ship for twelve consecutive days, through all the hours of daylight. It was long, hard, boring and eventually very tiring. Perhaps it was as well that by then we were already well into May, less than six weeks from the longest southern hemisphere winter night. Dawn was at about seven in the morning. By five in the afternoon it was starting to get dark. I steered for ten to fifteen hours at a stretch every day, breaking into my time at the tiller only to assemble some food for a cold picnic lunch on deck, and to take and reduce my celestial observations.

At night I devised all manner of wondrous sail plans to try to keep *Roc* heading in roughly the right direction and maintaining at least some minimal speed. As dusk fell I refilled and lit my little hurricane lamp and hung it from its hook on a coach-roof beam. It reflected off the varnished woodwork, making the cabin warm and welcoming. I ferreted around in the lockers to find the constituents for an evening meal. My stores were in total disarray after the capsize and most of the tinned food had lost its labels. With no cooking facilities, meal preparation was greatly simplified. I pulled out whatever came to hand until I had enough for a meal, and ate it. I drank water, neat or with Ship's lime juice added. That was it.

I then turned in to my bunk. I'd been gradually drying out sodden clothes and bedding in the drier weather, so had a warm and dry sleeping bag to crawl into. I had a reciprocating compass set into the bulkhead above my head, so could check our course while lying stretched out. At night this was mostly academic, as we were scarcely moving anyway.

My daily treat was then to listen to my transistor radio. By now I was losing the New Zealand stations and picking up Australia. I homed in on a few stations that I liked, with classical music, some jazz, some intelligent discussion. The sounds and voices wafted over me, re-establishing some connection with that other life on land, and without fail lulled me to sleep. I woke regularly to check the horizon for shipping, but this was an empty part of the ocean. In fact over the twenty-four day period between my close encounter with the Japanese fishing boat, and starting to meet more fishing boats off the Australian coast, I saw only one ship.

As light started to filter slowly into the cabin at about six thirty in the morning I got up, had some bread and jam for breakfast, cleaned my teeth, then hauled myself on deck for another long day at the helm. With no cockpit well I had just the flat deck to sit on. My course never changed. Two-ninety magnetic. Two-ninety magnetic. Every day, day after day. Two-ninety magnetic. My steering compass, housed in a specially built box just aft of the coach-roof, was a Bosun grid compass. At least it could be read quickly and easily from a distance. Where possible I steered by the sky or the sun.

Mid-morning, if the sun was visible, I hove to and took my a.m. sight, diving below to quickly work up a position line. Then back to the tiller. Always the hard deck and tiller. Two-ninety magnetic. Two-ninety magnetic. Lunch was an assortment of cold bits and pieces – cheese, salami, dates, apple, nuts – thrown into a bowl and eaten at the helm. I had another short break from the tyranny of the tiller as the sun neared its meridian altitude. Another sight, another dive below to work my latitude and bring forward my morning position line, another cross on the chart. My daily average was down to about sixty-five miles for this period. Then back once more to the tiller. Two-ninety magnetic. Two-ninety magnetic. On it went, hour after hour until dusk when I refilled and lit my little hurricane lamp and hung it from its hook on a coach-roof beam.

I found a score of ways to relieve the monotony and pass the time. I learned morse. I learned the international code of signals. I sang all the songs I knew. Out came the sea shanties. *In South Australia I was born. Heave away! Haul away! South Australia round Cape Horn. Bound for South Australia.* I made up new songs, long and complicated, mainly nonsensical, to while away the hours:

I've just seen a big white cloud
Somersault over my topmast shroud
As it looped the loop it yelled for joy
But it didn't have a parachute on.

Oh my! What to do,
Sailing along with a minimal crew.
Oh my! What to say
When you haven't got a parachute on.

I've just seen a crested wave
Dancing like an Indian brave.
One to the left and two to the right
But it didn't have its war-paint on.

Oh my! What to do
Sailing along with a minimal crew.
Oh my! What to say
When you haven't got your war-paint on.

And so on for hour after hour, round and round, and always holding two-ninety magnetic, two-ninety magnetic.

10

Sitting there day after day on the hard wooden deck I slowly realised that we were by no means alone. Two burgundy and silver striped pilot fish had adopted us. I became aware of them as they made little forays from under our bilges, grabbing something off the surface with a quick slap then darting back under the ship. I tried to train them by whistling, but they were resolutely unresponsive.

Later, when cruising the Barrier Reef, I found a suckerfish attached to the hull. Perhaps it too had taken up residence on this Tasman crossing. It was comforting to know we had regular company. We were now a sort of convoy heading north-west to Queensland. I became more self-important as a navigator. These fish were depending on me too.

One day two swallows landed on *Roc*. They were evidently heading the same way, but were totally exhausted. One perched on my now defunct wind vane. I slipped quietly below and came back on deck with my camera. Slowly I shuffled nearer to the fragile bundle of fluffed out feathers sitting quietly on the vane. It took no notice of me at all. I was finally so close that I couldn't focus my camera on it. If it had breathed hard it could have fogged up my lens. I took a few shots, using the last of my colour film. I went below again to reload my camera with some black and white film.

Standing with my head out of the companionway I suddenly heard a fluttering close to my ear and felt something on my head. The swallow had landed on my unruly and salty tangle of hair. It was a strange sensation to be six hundred miles offshore with a bird sitting on my head. *Nobody will ever believe me*, I thought.

Slowly, so as not to disturb my avian head-dress, I leaned forward and slid out a drawer that held a small hand mirror. I held it out in front of my face so that it reflected the swallow. With my other hand holding my camera I took several photographs, pointing the lens into the mirror. Proof for posterity. For a few minutes more we continued our impromptu liaison in statuesque immobility and mutual incomprehension. Then the bird, together with his, or her, mate, flew off, perhaps suicidally, over the sea, driven by their own imperatives to the western horizon.

I naturally assumed that I would have no more St Francis of Assisi moments. How often do wild birds just come and perch on you? A few days later I was out on deck on a very dark night adjusting the tiller when I became aware of a heavy fluttering overhead. In the soft light emanating from my hurricane lamp in the cabin I could just make out the shape of a large seabird hovering over the cockpit, just above my head. On an impulse I held up my forearm and pushed it gently into the bird's feet. It settled on my arm. *Well now*, I thought, *what do I do now?* The bird, about the size of a seagull, but sooty black all over except for a whiter patch on its forehead, seemed quite happy on its new perch. Had I missed a vocation as a falconer?

I had no intention of staying on deck all night, so I manoeuvred myself down into the cabin, with my new shipmate still balanced on my forearm. I settled it on a forward bunk and once again photographed the evidence. It stayed for most of the night, but was evidently not looking for a permanent relationship. Towards dawn it grew restless. I took it on deck and launched it gently skywards. Off it went into the night, leaving me once more to my solitude.

Sitting on deck, day after day, I spotted more and more elements of the oceanic wildlife: shearwaters, terns, petrels, black gannets, Portuguese men-of-war, flying fish, porpoises, dorados, dolphins. Best of all were the albatrosses. From time to time one would appear – they never seemed to keep company – and would wheel around the boat for hours in a breath-taking display of aeronautic mastery. They would never, ever have to move their wings, such was their ability as gliders, wheeling in and riding the updrafts from the swells, banking round with their wingtips a hair's breadth from the wave tops, always in total control of their flight path, not wasting an ounce of unnecessary energy, relaxed, unhurried, one of the supreme end-points of millions of years of evolutionary honing. I watched them for hours on end, mesmerised by their ceaseless pattern-making through the air, by their majestic effortlessness. Often *Roc* seemed to form the central axis of their orbiting, as they wove complex trails round and round the boat. What tiny spark of inquisitiveness impelled them to stick close, when they had a whole wide ocean to play on?

11

After twelve long days of hand steering, twelve days that brought me to a kind of harmony with the sea around me and my life upon it, conditions started to change. The wind came round more into the west. This in principle meant *Roc* could once more sail herself, but for days it was a flukey, fickle wind, up and down, round about. Several times my distance made good was little more than forty-five miles, despite endless tending of the boat to keep her sailing in the constantly shifting zephyrs.

A new worry was starting to creep in. The race organisers had set an official finishing limit of thirty days. With a fair wind I could still reach the Australian coast within this time limit. With this current mix of short squalls and long calms I could well miss the deadline. The thought was devastating. I had struggled on against the odds in order to be an official finisher in the race. It would be cruel to be denied even that.

About this time I heard a report on the radio that a thirty-eight-foot ferro-cement yacht was three weeks overdue on a Tasman crossing from Auckland to Queensland. Shipping and aircraft had been alerted to look out for it. That yacht was to haunt me weeks later when relatives of those on board contacted me, desperate for some crumb of hope that the yacht or its crew could still be found. I did hear a story, perhaps apocryphal, that, before leaving, the skipper had boasted of his navigational ignorance, claiming that to sail to Australia was easy – *You just sail up to the north of New Zealand, turn left and keep on going.* Would that were the case. In fact there are several severe hazards lying quietly in wait hundreds of miles off the Australian coast. Lord Howe Island, Ball's Pyramid and various rocky outcrops in their vicinity are fairly obvious. More subtle and menacing are two huge reefs to the north of the Lord Howe group – Middleton Reef and Elizabeth Reef. These are graveyards to innumerable ships. Even Bill Belcher, winner of this particular race, and a world-girdling navigator, sailed his yacht *Josephine* onto Middleton Reef four years later. He was lucky to escape with his life, boldly launching his life-raft off the reef and drifting until picked up by a freighter.

The days passed and I struggled slowly on. By the 25th May I had been at sea for twenty-eight days. I had two days left in which to finish, and was less than a hundred miles off the Australian coast. It was tantalisingly close. That day a fair wind came up from the west-south-west, almost a leading wind, blowing fifteen to twenty knots. My hopes started to rise again. Perhaps I may just scrape in within the time limit. I had eaten most of my food, drunk a good portion of my water. *Roc* was a little lighter and perhaps a little faster. At five that evening I passed two Japanese long-liners. We were moving back into soundings. However the wind continued to rise and by seven that evening was gusting to thirty knots. The barometer was falling rapidly. There was little doubt. Another storm was coming.

All night it blew harder and harder. By seven the next morning we were down to deep-reefed mainsail and storm jib, trying to keep up some progress to windward, in gusts of up to forty knots. I was getting concerned about my steering system once again. For nearly four weeks of ocean sailing the tiller had been bolted to a single cheek of quarter-inch mild steel. The steel, not surprisingly, was starting to show signs of fatigue at the critical point between the aft end of the cheek and the weld that held it to the sleeve on the rudder shaft. It was clear that it would now not take much more stress to snap it off completely.

However much I thought about it, I could not figure out what I could do if this happened. I needed to nurse the steering system as best I could. The sea conditions were building to a nasty state. This was hardly surprising, particularly as we were now moving into the influence of the south-flowing East Australian Current. As I wrote ruefully in my log that evening:

With a wind from the west, a current from the north, a swell from the south, and me from the east, things are pretty impossible.

We were now less than twenty-four hours from the official time limit for finishing. I had to accept the inevitable. We would not make it. It was a bitter disappointment, but I could not dwell on it. We were once again in severe storm conditions. There were more important priorities than a mere race. We were back to the more fundamental matter of survival.

12

The great Australian east coast storm of the night of 27-28th May 1974 is still remembered with awe. The May 2005 edition of the Australian online magazine Afloat carried, in its 'Do You Remember?' series, an article entitled 'When The 'Cyclone' Hit Sydney'. It starts thus:

> *On the morning of 28th May 1974, the good burghers of Sydney came out of their beds, turned on their radios, and then looked at their morning papers and blinked in amazement. During the night a massive storm had hit Sydney and coastal areas had taken the full blast. A large ship was aground north of Newcastle, several yachts were missing at sea with their crews probably dead, and the RAN destroyer escort HMAS Swan had carried out a very fine piece of seamanship to rescue a yacht's crew in 18m (60') seas hammered by 100 knot winds.*

The ship in question was a Swedish bulk carrier, whose back was broken in the heavy seas. Apart from the yacht *Cutty Sark*, whose crew was rescued by the Australian Navy destroyer escort, three other yachts were known to be at sea in the general area. *Nimbus II*, with a crew of three aboard, including a father and son, had been sailing in company with the *Cutty Sark*, but had become separated from her in the atrocious conditions. The yacht had sent a man overboard mayday. She was lost with all crew. The yacht *Elsie*, with two aboard, was lost with all crew. There was one other yacht known to be out there, a little chap with a crew of one. *Roc.*

Of course I was the only one who knew, more or less, where I was. I was by then about eighty miles offshore between Cape Moreton to the south and Double Island Point to the north. Despite the strong south-flowing current I had been forced, by the recent headwinds, fifty miles or so to the north of my ideal track. This was just as well – I was further than I otherwise would have been from the centre of the depression. The race organisers and other marine authorities on shore could only speculate as to where I actually was. Their understandable fear, with the carnage unrolling further south, was that I too was caught by the full force of the storm.

I listened regularly to the radio news broadcasts. A febrile atmosphere prevailed in respect of the missing yachts. Air searches were commenced. A body was washed up on the north coast of New South Wales. It was thought that it may well be that of a 'missing' single-handed sailor. Yes indeed. Yours truly. I sat on my bunk and listened to reports of my own death. It was a little alarming. Was there something I had missed in all this? Did those voices on the radio know something I didn't? I concluded, after some reflection, that I myself was probably best placed to decide whether I was alive or not. I consoled myself with the thought that the reports of my death were probably exaggerated.

I am also pretty certain I have been alive ever since. It has certainly felt like it, not that I'm an expert on the alternative. But now I'm not quite so sure. As I read down to the bottom of the Afloat article on the great Sydney 'cyclone', written thirty-one years after the event, I came across the following sentence:

That night the small (19ft) yacht Roc, *competing in a single-handed race from New Zealand to Australia, was lost together with her skipper.*

Damn.

In any event, the worst night of the storm in our sector was the previous night. It was evidently moving south. By the night in question in the article the winds north of Brisbane were down to twenty knots and falling. We were sailing again just slightly north of west. As morning broke we started to meet the most stupendous swells coming up from the south, no doubt the aftermath of the storm.

I have seen nothing like it before or since. These were not waves as we normally know them. They were huge, smooth, rolling hillsides. As near as I could estimate the distance between the highest points of each succeeding swell was close to a hundred yards. There was absolutely nothing threatening about the swells. They were enormously high, but the face of each was just a long smooth gradient. The tops were wide whalebacks. To go from the top of each swell, with its bird's-eye panorama, slowly down into the deep trough, then ride up, as on a sedate escalator, to the next crest, took the best part of a minute. It was hard to even start to contemplate the forces required to create such a monumental disturbance to the surface of the ocean.

The sea-state just of itself was extraordinary. But another element rendered it almost supernatural. In the top of every moving crest, as far as the eye could see in either direction, were hundreds and hundreds of dolphins, surfing easily in the wave energy, getting a free ride north. It was some sort of mass migration, literally on the back of the forces unleashed by the recent storm.

My noon position put us about thirty miles east of Double Island Point. By mid afternoon we were heading due west towards the coast in a light breeze from south-south-west. The sea started to smooth out and take on a strange choppy state, millions of tiny waves dancing upwards. We were entering the centre of the East Australian Current. It was like a river flowing along through the normal sea around it. For half an hour we moved across this hissing stream, then sailed out of it, back into the usual sea-state. The wind died further and by dusk we were becalmed.

For the whole night we lay slatting in the huge swells, going nowhere. Maybe it didn't matter now. We had missed our deadline. Time was immaterial. However I was increasingly worried about the tiller fitting. It looked as if it could fracture at any time. At dawn a tiny breeze came up, still from the south-south-west, and we ghosted towards the coast through the swells, still huge and occasionally still pushing along great lines of dolphins.

I knew land was near. I could smell it. A hot fragrance, all the multifarious scents of sub-tropical vegetation, mixed with the raw smell of the red, baked earth itself, wafted over the boat. I breathed deeply, filling my lungs with it, marvelling at its heady complexity after weeks of exposure to the arid, slightly acidic smell of the sea. At ten that morning, just three hours short of thirty-two days at sea, the low blue-grey line of the Queensland coast rose gently above the horizon. A terse entry in my log said simply:

No excitement – only dull relief.

We had almost crossed the Tasman Sea, against so many odds, but, as the *Endeavour II* experience had shown, there can be a world of difference between 'almost' and 'actually'.

13

The narrow entrance to Port Cartwright, the sea-going end of Mooloolaba, end point of this voyage, was still fifty miles or so to the south. With the light winds now blowing from that direction, there was still work to do. Within a couple of hours of sighting land we lay once more becalmed in the swell, under a comforting warm sun. I dragged out all my damp clothes and bedding, spreading them around the deck to air and dry them. Out of the distance came a dull roar. It quickly grew louder and louder. I looked hastily around but could see nothing. On it came. What the hell was going on? Tidal wave? What on earth...?

With a heart-stopping, deafening whoosh a fighter plane, until then hidden behind the mainsail, shot over us a hundred feet above the mast. After a month of nothing but the soft-edged sounds of nature, my ears nearly exploded as the zillion decibels of the two jet engines hit us. The plane reared skywards, then banked and came hurtling back, strafing us with another round of imminent deafness. Despite the monumental fright the plane had given me on its first pass, I was relieved to see it. No doubt it would report the sighting and our position. This turned out to be the case. Over the next twenty-four hours we had visits from a number of planes, ranging from a big RAAF transport to a two-seater.

However progress along this last leg of the voyage was

still painfully slow. We tacked down the coast through a mess of thundery squalls and calms. The next afternoon a Queensland prawn trawler, the *Wave Crest*, overtook us and offered a tow. *Thanks mate but no.* For yet another night we struggled south through gyrating squalls and great empty holes, devoid of wind. The morning sun disappeared as low cloud drove in from the south-west. The barometer began another descent.

By mid-morning of the last day of May, my thirty-fourth day at sea, and just a few miles from our destination, we were wrapped in a misty mantle of driving rain in a near gale. Visibility was down to a few hundred yards, the land long since swallowed up in the low cloud. Neither of the tactical choices for our course was appealing. Port tack took us in towards the land and danger. Starboard tack took us away from danger, but away from our goal. That afternoon I stood in as far as I dared towards the coast, then tacked seawards again and hove to. I knew that Port Cartwright was somewhere just there a few miles to the west. There was nothing for it but to wait for clearer weather before closing the coast for, hopefully, the final time.

Hove-to in twenty-five knot winds and a lumpy sea, I turned in and slept. There was little point keeping a watch – there was nothing to see. At three in the morning I was forced out of my deep sleep by a blinding bright light shining through the port-lights. I struggled up through the hatch to see what was going on. A forty-foot pilot boat, the *John Oxley*, was lying a few yards to windward, its searchlight blazing at us. Further to windward I could just make out the slab sides of a merchant ship, the *Hong Kong Success*, providing us with a lee from the wind.

The Brisbane River pilot boats are based in Mooloolaba, just to the north of the Moreton Bay entrance, where they can get in and out quickly to the merchant traffic they serve.

The *John Oxley* passed me a line, which I was now quite happy to accept. To have refused a tow for the few remaining miles, given the conditions, would have been both churlish and foolhardy. We set off at a good lick, more than I considered comfortable, and headed land-wards.

As dawn broke the coastline, now just a mile to starboard, came into sharp focus in the clearing weather. What an intoxicating brew of sights and smells! The inimitable perfume of an Australian dawn, so familiar from my months spent in the outback, filled my lungs. Land! The subtle colours and contours of the coastal hinterland were a kaleidoscopic visual wonder after weeks and weeks of just sea and sky, sky and sea.

A small launch came alongside and put aboard John McFarlane, the commodore of the Mooloolaba Yacht Club. The bush telegraph had been working overtime. I grasped his hand and gratefully devoured the sandwiches and hot soup he had thoughtfully brought with him. Ah! A hot drink! At last a hot drink!

We came through the narrow entrance between the moles of Port Cartwright. I realised then how hard that entrance would have been to find for the first time in anything but the best conditions. Up the narrow river we went for another mile or so to Mooloolaba itself, where we turned to starboard, cast off our tow, and tied *Roc* alongside the yacht club jetty.

It was eight o'clock in the morning of 1st June. I had been at sea for just under thirty-five days and logged 2173 nautical miles. Despite the early hour a big crowd had already gathered. It seemed our arrival was, in its own little way, news. No doubt the recent storm, with its loss of life, rescues, searches, damage both at sea and on shore, had added an edge to the public interest. It seemed there were many who just wanted a first-hand look at this tiny yacht, the smallest ever to have made it across from New Zealand.

A stack of messages and telegrams was thrust into my hand. As I read them I answered questions from the reporters who had already arrived. I tidied up the deck and stowed my sails, pausing to pose for a photo now and then. I was very tired, but hyperactive with the stimulus of arrival and this sudden unexpected babble of human voices.

Once *Roc* was as shipshape as I could make her I stepped uncertainly ashore and was taken up to the already crowded yacht club by John. It was by now about ten o'clock. *Fancy a beer, mate?* asked John. A beer. The local equivalent of the English 'nice cup of tea'. How could I say no? The cameras flashed once again as I downed my glass of icy cold intoxicant. Next up was a hot meal – steak, eggs and salad. Luxury!

By now the pressure was telling on me. I desperately needed sleep. One of the Pilot Service deckhands, Dave Quirke, a big blond Englishman with a comforting London River accent, lived just over the road from the yacht club with his wife Alison. They kindly offered me their spare room. By mid-afternoon, after a long and scalding hot shower, I was asleep, cocooned in a warm, soft, dry and strangely stable bed.

Sleep. I fell into the longest and deepest sleep of my life. For seventeen hours my systems closed down as I descended into the recuperative depths. The stress and strain and fears and discomforts of the last month ebbed away and I floated off into a black mist of happy forgetfulness. We had arrived. For the ocean sailor that is all, really, that ever matters.

Postscript

Roc and I covered many more thousands of ocean miles together, including a return crossing of the Tasman Sea. Having tested our mettle to the limits, nature from then on left us alone. Almost all our subsequent voyaging was in relatively benign conditions. I fashioned a new servo-pendulum oar for the self-steering gear in Mooloolaba. This one saw out my time with *Roc*.

When we left Mooloolaba, after a few weeks of recuperation and repairs, to cruise north to the Great Barrier Reef, we had a crewmember aboard. *Roc* largely owed her existence to the kindness and support of Don Gaskell, the farmer on whose land she was built. Don loved the water, but had never done any 'proper' sailing. As a thank you to him I invited him to sail with us for the first leg of our next journey up the Queensland coast.

Don and I had spent much of our time together, over the previous few years, discussing every question that life threw up, usually while leaning idly over a farm gate watching his livestock munching the grass. After a working life spent out on his own, tending his land and stock – he had previously farmed a remote coastal block – Don loved to test out his ideas against another mind prepared to think and argue with him. Don had the wisdom and wit born of a lifetime on the land. Sailors often disparage 'farmers', but both are subject to the cycles of nature, and develop a similar mind-set. We had become the greatest of friends.

We sailed for a week or so up the coast, to the southern end of the reef. The sun shone. We swam with the dolphins in tranquil indigo seas. We sailed close past the southernmost coral cay – Lady Elliot Island – with its blinding white shore-line and swaying palms. A balmy south-easterly wafted us north to Gladstone. We picked up a pile mooring just off the town and there Don left us.

Three weeks later he was dead, drowned in an accident while fishing on Lake Taupo, back in New Zealand. His lit-tle cabin cruiser had hit a floating object as he and two friends crossed the lake. All three were thrown out into the deep waters far from the shore. The two younger men with him were eventually rescued. Don, a good swimmer, was never seen again. It is thought that perhaps he was injured as he was thrown out.

I learned of this reading a telegram from one of his daughters, Moira, in the Gladstone post office. Overcome, I let out a great wail. My best mate was gone. Drowned. Of all things – drowned! The ironies were cruel and obvious, and yet another lesson on the blind indifference of fate.

Roc *in frame in her shed. The shed was later completely enclosed.*

Fairing the temporary frames.

Roc *almost ready for plastering.*

A strong coach roof!

View from forward, showing the shapely coachroof and wide side decks.

Loading Roc *for transport to Auckland.*

Almost afloat!

*Roc at New Plymouth prior to the start of the 1974
Single-handed Trans-Tasman Race.*

Fair weather in the Tasman Sea

Roc *in heavy weather, mid-Tasman, with a smashed self-steering gear and jury main steering.*

PART THREE

CALMS

Alone, alone, all, all alone,
Alone on a wide, wide sea!
Unless this wind picks up damn soon
We won't be home for tea...

Extract from the log of *Mingming*, 1430 hours,
22nd June 2006

1

I had been vaguely thinking of doing another ocean voyage for a while. I was getting in plenty of sailing, but just the usual weekend sallies up the river, sometimes up the coast, and back. Once a year Brenda and I would try and get in a week's cruising, along the east coast from our base, in Burnham-on-Crouch, to the Suffolk rivers and back. Nothing adventurous. It suited us. We were both working very hard, and were quite happy to spend most of the time relaxing at anchor.

Our yacht, *Mary Ellen,* a 10 ton gaff cutter, had been bought for nothing more than east coast pottering. She had been built in Brightlingsea in 1934 by the smack builders Kidby & Sons. I had found her at Birdham Pool, in Chichester Harbour, and sailed her back to Burnham, where I now had a house. With the help of Mark Butler of James Lawrence Sailmakers of Brightlingsea, and Priors Boatyard in Burnham, she was converted back to her original gaff rig. Under full sail she was an impressive sight and a powerful sailor.

However she was not a boat I would use for blue water voyaging. Too old; too big for easy single-handing; with her long boom, unsuited to using a wind vane; lacking a self-draining cockpit, and so on. No, what I needed was another small, strong and easily-handled yacht in which, if I could find the time, I could sneak off to sea now and again.

I was interested in the possibilities of junk rig and had been to look at a junk-rigged Kingfisher 20, *Fei Fan*, that was for sale up the river at Althorne. I was also playing around with designs of my own for possible building, and had built a three-foot model of a shallow draught sharpie-type hull. There was no doubt I was getting restless. For many years I had managed to evade the pull of the horizon. But I was getting withdrawal symptoms. I needed another fix. This I knew, but I couldn't seem to find the right peg to hang my restlessness on.

Then I read about the Jester Challenge. Here was a new transatlantic race with no rules and no nannies, designed to bring ocean racing back to its roots, to re-enfranchise the small-boat sailor, and to revive the simple principle of total skipper responsibility. A little pyrotechnic display went off in my head. I could not imagine anything more suited to my history and temperament, and more suited to the need I had at that moment for another ocean challenge. There was no doubt, no hesitation, no mulling over, no second thoughts. I knew as soon as I read the short yachting magazine article that I would participate. This was just what I was looking for, just the stimulus to focus my energies and get me to sea again.

I immediately contacted the owner of *Fei Fan*, but she was by then sold. Ideally, I would have liked to have built my own yacht again, for all the same reasons I built *Roc*, but the problem was time. There was less than a year to the proposed start date of the Jester Challenge. Building a boat, and preparing it for sea, in that time scale, while still running a demanding business, was out of the question. My strategy was therefore to try to find a suitable small second-hand yacht, preferably devoid of sophisticated 'kit', and without an inboard engine, that I could quickly strip out and rebuild, using the simple principles for seaworthiness that I had been thinking about for so many years.

I was also keen that if possible the yacht should be junk-rigged. It was again quite a coincidence that having already been considering buying a junk-rigged yacht, the Jester Challenge, named after the most famous junk-rigged yacht of all, and based on 'Blondie' Hasler's proposals for a Transatlantic Series Two race, should be the catalyst for this third adventure.

I doubt that a junk-rigged bilge-keeled Corribee, just under twenty-one feet long, is many people's idea of the perfect ocean cruiser. For me she was ideal. I found *Mingming*, or *Phaedra* as she then was, laid up ashore at Woodbridge. The owners, Brian and Margaret Gascoine, had already bought a bigger yacht and were keen to sell. We agreed a price about an hour after I first saw her.

What was the attraction? For a start she had a Hasler-style junk rig, and so felt right for the Jester Challenge. I liked the tight, strength-giving compound curvature of the Corribee hull. She had low freeboard, reducing windage and lateral resistance to breaking waves. For my money, the shallow draft was good for both coastal sailing and blue water work – a light boat with a deep keel can easily be tripped and capsized if thrown sideways by a breaking sea; shallow draft reduces this possibility.

The junk-rigged Corribees were the only Corribees built with small, seamanlike port-lights rather than big cabin windows. This one had no inboard engine, satisfyingly defunct electrics, a chemical head that could be scrapped, the original spirit stove – I'd long since stopped having gas on small boats, and no unnecessary toys – no VHF, no GPS, no log, no depth-sounder, no nothing. Just what I wanted – an uncomplicated boat that I could build up from scratch to my own specification.

It was very obvious that she could be altered quickly and easily – especially the cockpit and hatch area – to make her properly seaworthy. The large lazaret was perfect for creating aft foam buoyancy; there was a mass of space under the cockpit floor where more foam could go, and it would be a simple matter to install a watertight bulkhead forward to enclose yet more flotation.

For the previous ten years she had only been sailed on the Deben River, so was relatively unused. Finally, although on that particular day I was tired and couldn't be bothered with too much haggling, she didn't cost much. This was important. I had set myself a very stringent budget for this whole venture. Ocean racing, and maybe ocean sailing in general, has become a chequebook sport. I wanted to do this on the minimum outlay.

I sailed *Mingming* down from the Deben in a squally Force 6 north-westerly. It was the first time I had ever sailed with a junk rig. I was immediately impressed with its ease of handling. More than that, it is a rig that can be sailed, always, for the wind you've got, not the wind you might get in fifteen or thirty minutes. As the squalls came in I could drop a panel or two of the sail, from the cockpit, simply by releasing the main halyard. Once the squall had passed I could haul up the reefed panels in a second or two.

It was a novel and wonderful feeling to have no anxiety whatsoever about getting caught carrying too much sail. Moreover I quickly discovered that the junk rig did not press the boat hard. The fairly flat, fully-battened sail worked perfectly efficiently almost feathering into the wind, reducing the heeling moment considerably. Off the wind *Mingming* was fast, but for the final windward beat into Burnham into a backing westerly, much less impressive.

Nonetheless I was delighted with this maiden sail. I knew I had a lot to learn about the rig, and how to get the most out of it, but I had immediately felt totally at ease with it. Similarly the Corribee overall had behaved impeccably; light and responsive on the helm, quite untroubled in the nasty short seas through the Spitway, buoyant and reassuring. It was clear the Corribee's reputation as an excellent little sea-boat was well-deserved. I was confident I had made a good choice and could move on to the next stage of the preparation process.

2

I sailed *Mingming* hard for a few more weeks, all the while checking the practicality of the changes I was about to make. At the end of September she was hauled out for a rapid-fire rebuild. I took a week or so off work and enlisted the help of my good friend Darren Noonan, a talented young Burnham shipwright who often crewed for us on *Mary Ellen*. We got stuck in and within ten days had transformed *Mingming* from a standard Corribee into a mean and purposeful ocean mini-cruiser, strong, totally watertight and unsinkable.

A watertight bulkhead was put in just forward of the forward end of the coach-roof. Apart from the chain locker, the whole area forward of the bulkhead was filled tight with closed-cell foam. The after bulkhead was made watertight, the lazaret emptied and filled with foam, and its hatch sealed down. Prior to that the mountings for the Windpilot self-steering gear were fitted to the transom.

The cockpit well was more than halved in size by the addition of a large watertight locker at the after end. We replaced the main hatch washboards with solid mahogany, recycled from an old table, bringing back memories of the building of *Roc*. A further raised bridge-deck was fitted above the existing one. We removed the sliding hatch and replaced it with a proper watertight hatch. Further foam was added under the cockpit floor. My calculations suggested that by then *Mingming* had about 150% of the flotation required to keep her where one would like to be kept – on the surface of the ocean.

I took out the clever but totally unnecessary fold-down Corribee sink, building shelves into the now empty locker space to house my sextant, deck watch and other navigation equipment. Most of the running rigging was replaced and a spare main halyard fitted. Darren built me a couple of fifteen-foot Douglas fir sculling oars, to double also as jury steering oars and jury mast. I installed LED navigation lights powered by a gel battery, itself charged by a small flexible solar panel fitted to the coach-roof. These were the only electrics on board.

Finally, heavy bronze chain-plates, salvaged from the refitting of *Mary Ellen*, were attached with three half-inch bolts each to the after end of the topsides to serve as attachment points for the series drogue I was planning to make over the winter. I had learned my lesson on *Roc* and would this time make sure I had good streaming gear. The outboard engine that had come with *Mingming*, and which I had used just once to leave the rather tight mooring at Woodbridge, had long since been brought ashore and laid up in my garage.

Within a few weeks a transformed *Mingming* was back afloat, ready for a winter of hard sailing and trials. I love winter sailing. It's a treat to have all the waterways almost to yourself. The river-clogging moorings are empty, creating a spaciousness and freedom that disappears in summer. Of course it is cold, but I like the solid feel of the denser cold winter wind. The bird life on the rivers and mudflats takes on proportions never seen in summer, with huge and cacophonously wheeling flocks of wintering waders, ducks and geese. I also wanted to do as much night sailing as possible, to relearn the particular skills and rhythm that go with it. The long, long winter nights were ideal for that.

I spent many winter weekends creeping about the east coast at night, sometimes in pitch blackness, other times under a crisp full moon. The deck was often iced up, but wearing thermal underwear, several guernseys, my ski trousers and jacket, with waterproofs over them for good measure, and topped off with a Russian-style imitation fur hat, I rarely got too cold. That winter was notable for its constant procession of high-pressure systems, so I had predominantly settled, clear weather. I did not get as much heavy weather exposure as I would have liked. Nonetheless there was no doubt that when I started the difficult haul down to Plymouth, in mid April, I was fully prepared both physically and psychologically.

I left Burnham-on-Crouch on the morning of 14th April 2006, Good Friday, bound as far as I could get over the long weekend. I was still working, so would have to make the voyage to Plymouth in weekend stages. I did not want to leave my journey to the West Country too late. The start of the Jester Challenge was scheduled for 3rd June, and I wanted to be well along the south coast by mid May.

A gentle westerly gave *Mingming* an easy passage across the Thames estuary, but the weather started to deteriorate as we exited Fisherman's Gat at dusk. I rang Brenda to tell her where we were and described the bright lights of Margate and the north Kent coast ahead. I put the 'phone away and looked south again. Nothing! The lights had been switched off! I checked our heading on the compass. On course. What the...? A minute or two later we were wrapped up tight in as thick a fog as I have known; a solid, smelly, invasive, horrible fog.

There was still just enough breeze to keep us moving and we edged gently south towards the North Foreland. The wind died to almost nothing. The fog gripped tighter. Through the gloom a ghostly glow, underpinned by a regular humming, moved slowly closer. Then another. We were drifting through the ships at anchor in Margate Roads. With some help from the ebb tide I got some offing, and took a short nap. It dawned as grey as a politician's suit, the fog still heavy, but with a breeze starting to pipe up from the east. Off we set south inside the Goodwins, with a freshening beam wind and a fair tide.

Round the South Foreland we went, though we had a good offing and never saw it. Past Dover, lost too in the fog, running the gauntlet of the honking ferries, all well hidden in the murk. With the wind now dead aft, the self-steering comfortably settled, on we sped west, with never a sight of land. An invisible Dungeness came and went. By midnight we were south of Beachy Head, stalled by the flood tide and a wind that had maliciously gone round to the south-west.

As Easter Sunday dawned I closed the land on port tack, coming in to the Seven Sisters cliffs to the west of Beachy Head, the first land I had seen since the fog had rolled in thirty-six hours previously. I hoped to beat up to Brighton on the ebb tide. It was not to be. The wind died to almost nothing. I tacked offshore again, not wanting to be too close in to Beachy Head in a failing breeze. The tide turned and, as we were carried back east, a hazy Eastbourne was opened up. I had now been sailing for over two days with not much sleep. The south-westerly started to freshen, so I eased the sheet and ran down to Eastbourne and into Sovereign Yacht Harbour. The guys there were extremely helpful, giving *Mingming* a tow into the lock, and then to her berth. We were on our way.

3

Two weeks later it was the May Bank Holiday weekend. I caught the train down to Eastbourne after work, and by eight on Friday evening was aboard *Mingming*. My plan was to leave the yacht harbour at about one o'clock the next morning, to catch the ebb tide west and get a good start for the next leg. I had a couple of hours' sleep, then sculled *Mingming* round to the holding pontoon near the locks. The lock-keeper had advised that there was another yacht locking out at that time, and they would be happy to throw me a line and tow me out of the entrance channel.

Just before two, on a black moonless night, the yacht *Annaliese*, bound for Dieppe, slipped the towrope, and headed off south-east into the gloom. With a light northerly breeze and the tide under us, we were soon round Beachy Head and on course for the Looe Channel. By dawn the wind had strengthened a little and Brighton, so elusive two weeks previously, was already abeam. On we went in the increasing sunshine, ticking off each of those resonant south coast names – Shoreham, Littlehampton, Worthing, Bognor... Bognor! Now we're getting somewhere!

The wind failed as we exited the Looe Channel. The tide was setting us towards Boulder Bank, an unwelcoming mass of angrily hissing wavelets, so I anchored to hold our position and wait for some wind. This was not long coming – a good fresh breeze from south-south-east. We were soon under way again, and by dusk had the Portsmouth forts well in our sights. Again the wind failed, and with the tide now against us, it was impossible to make progress. We worked our way slowly south, out of the main shipping channel, through the ships anchored in St Helen's Roads, to anchor at about midnight just off St Helen's Fort.

By half five the next morning we were under way again in a brisk breeze from north-north-east, under full main and my little nylon multi-purpose genoa to give us a bit more drive. The tide was starting to flood, but we continued to make steady progress, passing No Man's Land Fort by seven thirty. Gradually hundreds and hundreds of yachts appeared, all heading east on the flood tide, a typical Solent swarm, many probably on the first weekend cruise of the season. There seemed only to be *Mingming*, attracting curious stares at her strange rig, gamely stemming the tide.

By midday the wind had gone completely. I anchored off Osborne Bay, out of place amongst the Sunday picnickers, to wait for the west-going last of the flood. A small breeze finally sprang up from the east, so I got my anchor and, with some tide now under us, headed round to our next stopping point at East Cowes.

Mingming had now covered half the distance from Burnham-on-Crouch to Plymouth, but I was by no means complacent about the task still facing us. Ahead lay a string of tide-gates, difficult for a small and engine-less sailing craft to breach. Portland Bill, in particular, with its fierce tides and massive race, hung in the forefront of my mind.

The wind had gone into the south-west just as we arrived at Cowes, and it stuck there, with varying degrees of ferocity, for most of May. I had been hoping to get in one more weekend leg before linking up permanently with *Mingming*, but south-westerly gales put paid to that.

Brenda and I went down to East Cowes to spend a weekend on the yacht, as I had some work to do on her. In particular I had decided to replace the original Electrolux double burner spirit stove with a new Optimus single burner unit. I had taken the original, a wonderfully quirky and, when working properly, efficient invention, out of the yacht and serviced it, but it was still too unpredictable, if not downright dangerous. As it turned out, I never regretted dispensing with it. Apart from the total reliability of the replacement, I also gained some very useful additional galley space, as it was half the size of its predecessor.

That weekend we also started experimenting with my idea for even more buoyancy in *Mingming*. Most of my stores were to be carried in large watertight flare containers, lashed to the cabin sole and under the companionway. This meant that there was quite a lot of unused space under bunks. Rather than leave this space simply to fill with water and weigh down the boat even more in the event of a holing, I decided to fill it with extra movable flotation.

For several months we had been saving all our plastic containers – milk bottles, shampoo bottles and so on. At Cowes we started the next stage – filling them with expanding foam. This was to ensure that even if the tops were not watertight, they would still provide additional flotation and reduce the amount of water ingress. It took a while to get the hang of it – once out of its canister the foam keeps expanding, and expanding, and expanding. Then it starts *really* expanding. At first we badly overestimated how much foam should be put in each container. Cleaning up the sticky surplus that kept on issuing from each bottle was a horribly messy job.

When we arrived on that Saturday morning, *Mingming* was moored on her own, on an inside berth at the seaward end of the marina – tiny and a little forlorn. As the day progressed more and more big cruising yachts, most of them in excess of forty feet, filled up the berths, mainly two abreast, until little *Mingming* was totally dwarfed by the cliff-like topsides bearing down all around her. It was a Cruising Association rally. There was much hilarity and socialising all around. We quietly got on with our tasks, pretty much unnoticed among the expensive hardware surrounding us. By midday on Sunday we were on our own again. At one point at the height of the social activity I had thought of raising my Cruising Association pennant, but decided that anonymity is a sweet companion, and desisted.

4

The bad weather in the Channel continued, giving no opportunity to continue on west. On 19th May I finished work and started the long service leave (which, as the boss, I had magnanimously awarded myself) that gave me the time to participate in the Jester Challenge. I rejoined *Mingming*, and for several days lay on in East Cowes, listening to the heavy south-westerlies whistling in the shrouds and rattling the halyards in the marina. I was starting to get worried, as time was running out before the start. There was still a lot to do. All the main provisions for the voyage were still in London, waiting to be delivered to Plymouth.

On Tuesday 23rd I couldn't stand staying immobile in the marina any longer. The forecast was not good – south-west 5/7 – but I just had to get moving. I warped *Mingming* to the outside pontoon, and at nine thirty that morning left at the turn of the tide under full sail. My plan was to anchor in the lee of Hurst Castle, ready for a break in the weather. There was the possibility of a north-west change, according to the forecast. After a wet and uncomfortable sail up the Solent in a steep wind-over-tide chop, I anchored close in to the north-west of Hurst Castle, just before two in the afternoon. For a while we were very comfortable there. I was pleased to be away from the marina and on the move at last.

Overnight, conditions deteriorated, as the wind

increased to a near gale. The anchorage became less and less tenable. With a considerable scend starting to work its way round from the Needles Channel and a gusting wind screaming across the narrow spit of sand to windward, *Mingming* became less and less settled, snubbing angrily at her anchor warp. I was worried about any mishap that may cause the loss of my anchor, as I had taken my kedge ashore in Burnham to reduce weight for the Atlantic crossing. I was now regretting it, and wished I'd waited until Plymouth. At four that morning I decided it would be safer to retreat, so I got the anchor, with some difficulty in the conditions, and ran back to take refuge in Osborne Bay. By half six I was once more at anchor, this time in well-sheltered conditions.

The forecast was now for southerly gales, so I felt I had made the right decision. Having spent most of the night on anchor watch, it was a treat to get my head down for a few hours. Later in the day I took advantage of being in shallow water to dry *Mingming* out and give her a good scrub down. She had spent most of the last five weeks in marinas and a thin coat of slime had developed.

The next day dawned bleak and gusty, with a discouraging forecast – west 5/6 backing south-west 5/7, 8 later. Just the job for a nice sail down-Channel! Not being one to hang around, I decided nonetheless to have a second attempt at exiting the Solent and at least getting us to Studland Bay. My idea was to try to get to Hurst Castle as near as possible to the top of the tide, and if possible catch the whole of the ebb to Studland Bay. If it blew up too hard, I would just have to turn tail again.

By six in the morning we were under way under full mainsail and my small jib, making slow progress against wind and tide in grey, showery weather. As the flood started to reverse direction west we picked up speed and by eleven o'clock had passed Yarmouth. I felt optimistic. The cloud was breaking up, sending shafts of sunlight onto the Isle of Wight hills. At midday we shot past Hurst Castle in a tumultuous race and steered hard to starboard into North Channel. Suddenly we were out of the turbulence and roaring west, close inshore, with a fine leading wind. The strong ebb tide, now sparkling merrily under a bright sun, carried us west at a good lick for five hours. Bliss! As the tide turned we were well past Bournemouth, with Old Harry in sight and Studland Bay opening up to the south-west.

The wind died, and our forward progress died with it. Worse still, banks of thick fog were rolling in over the Isle of Wight astern and Swanage to the south. The 1756 hours forecast was for south-west 5/7, with fog banks. Studland Bay, such a good anchorage in westerly weather, seemed increasingly out of reach as the flood tide strengthened. Perhaps I could creep into Poole Harbour.

A late reprieve came in the form of an unexpected evening breeze out of the north-west. There was now no problem laying Studland Bay. By eight in the evening we were moored up to one of the sturdy pub courtesy buoys, with just one other yacht for company. I had no means of getting ashore, apart from swimming, so had to forego the obligatory fee of a pint or two. It had been a long but satisfying sail, forcing us along just that bit closer to Plymouth. I was ravenously hungry, having had little chance to eat during the day. After a hearty meal I was soon fast asleep.

The next day I lay in Studland Bay, resting, doing chores and maintenance, growing frustrated, wondering if the thumping squalls leaping down off the hills to windward would ever ease. The shipping forecasts repeated an unchanging litany of near gales, gales, rain and fog. There were now just eight days left before the Jester Challengers were due to cross the starting line off Plymouth Breakwater.

That evening the wind eased a little. I wasted no time in

slipping the mooring and heading off round Old Harry and past Swanage. By midnight we were well south of Anvil Point, bucking to windward with the tide under us. One by one the mainsail panels were reefed as the wind got up again to its habitual Force 7. We forced our way slowly west through the nasty black night. At the turn of the tide we were about ten miles south of Portland Bill. Day dawned in rough and unpleasant conditions, with a noxious-smelling fog all around. Little by little most of the gains of the night were eroded as the heavy seas and flood tide forced us back.

I felt quite dispirited. What the hell was I doing here? Why on earth had I so wanted to get back to sea? What made me think I could sail this little boat anywhere? The near gale continued. The fog banks, so loaded with pollutants that they looked almost rust-coloured, rolled chokingly across the relentless wave-tops. I knew that without a change of conditions, I would just yo-yo back and forth, making just a few miles on each ebb tide. It was no use expending my energy so ineffectively.

By early afternoon, with a very heavy heart, and wondering seriously if I still had the mettle required for this kind of tough solo sailing, I threw in the towel and wore round to run back to the shelter of Studland Bay. We headed back north-east with a following wind throwing up a big sea against the ebb spring tide. I set a course for St Alban's Head and Anvil Point, somewhere ahead in the heavy fog.

It suddenly struck me that, if I were somehow to dredge up the will to carry on with this whole enterprise, I now had a perfect opportunity to really test *Mingming's* sea-keeping abilities. Better to find out now if she had serious shortcomings than somewhere in mid-Atlantic. I decided to pass closer to the headlands than I would normally, to take *Mingming* through the over-falls, and see how she got on.

As we slowly closed the land the seas grew steeper, their

crests more urgent. I did not entrust *Mingming* to the self-steering gear. I had to do this myself, to feel her reactions and play her on the wave faces. Soon we were in the hissing overfalls. I battened down the main hatch and made sure my harness was attached to two strong points. Just two panels of the mainsail were set, but in the near gale our speed through the water was almost more than I would have liked.

Mingming handled the conditions with ease. She did not like to run absolutely straight to the waves crests, which tended to pick her up and surf her forward, risking loss of control and a broach. As soon as the angle to the following sea was reduced by ten or fifteen degrees, so that she was running very slightly obliquely down the wave face, she became reassuringly sedate in her handling.

I started to enjoy myself again. I now felt confident enough to give *Mingming* a more severe test by deliberately putting her beam on to a breaking crest. I chose my moment and put the helm down to bring her across a steep wave face. Over she went onto her beam ends. I had expected that she would stay down, recovering slowly. To my amazement, she snapped up immediately. The whole thing lasted scarcely two seconds. *OK, my girl,* I thought. *You'll do.*

For the third time in three days we passed that faithful sentinel, Old Harry, and beat into the bay to anchor, almost exactly twenty-four hours since slipping our mooring there. The weekend crowd had moved in, but with our shallow draft we were able to find an isolated spot close in to the cliffs. It was depressing to be back there again, forced eastwards for the second time in a few days. Plymouth seemed, at that moment, almost unattainable. On the other hand I had given *Mingming* her most rigorous sea trial so far, and been heartened by her response. I knew that she was up to the job in hand. The more pertinent question was – was I? After a quick meal I fell into a heavy sleep.

By nine the next morning I had got the anchor and was heading yet again past Old Harry. The north-westerly change had come, bringing clear skies, sunshine, and restoring my usual optimism. What a different day! Once round Anvil Point, with a crisp breeze just forward of the beam and the coastline in sharp focus, *Mingming* drove steadily westwards. The flood tide was no longer a barrier to progress. With the ebb under us we positively raced. I set a course to pass about eight miles south of Portland Bill and by midnight the regular sweep of the lighthouse beam was already well astern. All the next day we swept on across Lyme Bay in a freshening north-westerly. By late afternoon Start Point was almost abeam, three miles to the north, as we forced our way slowly forward over the flood tide.

Night fell and for the first time I saw the loom of the famous Eddystone light. The lights of Salcombe came and went in the dark and as day dawned there, at last, was the Devon coast stretching away north-west to Plymouth. After so much contrary weather and so much fog hiding the coastline, virtually since the North Foreland, the Devon cliffs and hills and bays and inlets, with their soft green-blue colourings in the slightly hazy morning air, were a welcome relief. As we opened up Plymouth Sound the wind fell away, but I didn't care. We were there. The difficult journey from the Essex mudflats to the Atlantic approaches had been accomplished.

At ten o'clock a strong and gusty northerly came up and I started the long beat into Plymouth, against wind and tide. Again, I felt no urgency. As we tacked our way doggedly through the eastern entrance every board gave me something new to look at: the navy frigates mooching slowly in and out of the western entrance, the lighthouse, the breakwater, the anchored merchant ships, and the town itself coming gradually into focus, the great shoulder of Plymouth Hoe dominating almost straight ahead.

Up we went to the mouth of the Cattewater and into Queen Anne Battery marina. The visitors' pontoon was already loaded with serious-looking yachts sporting an array of wind vanes – most of the other Jester Challengers were already assembled. It was midday on Tuesday. In exactly four days' time we would be setting out across the north Atlantic. The tribulations of the last week suddenly seemed trivial, almost banal. The real trials were yet to come.

5

The Jester Challenge was the typically bold idea of the retired lieutenant-colonel of Royal Marines Ewen Southby-Tailyour. Among his many achievements, both on and off the water, was the authorship of a fine biography of 'Blondie' Hasler. Ewen's father had been a co-officer with Hasler, and, as a child, Ewen had sailed with him. Hasler was the driving force behind the first transatlantic single-handed races and the designer of the modified junk-rigged folkboat *Jester*, which he sailed in them. With some sponsorship and backing from the Observer newspaper, the race, held every four years, became the Observer Single-handed Transatlantic Race – the OSTAR, as it is still called.

Its success as a sporting event soon surpassed anything Hasler could have imagined. In particular the involvement of a number of the great French single-handers, sailing bigger and bigger yachts specially designed and built for the race, pushed it to unforeseen levels of competitiveness and scale. The levels of publicity generated by the race attracted growing numbers of prospective entrants. The main results of all this were two-fold. Firstly the rules were made more and more complex and restrictive, in an attempt to limit the number of competitors. Secondly the smaller boats, that naturally took much longer to finish, were increasingly seen as a nuisance, irrelevant to the true spirit of the race.

By the time that the fifth race had been sailed, in 1976, 'Blondie' Hasler himself considered that the race had been 'killed by over-organisation'. Ever the creative one, the inveterate inventor, he formulated the outline of a Series Two transatlantic race, with the idea that it would be run in 1980. The new principles would cleanse the race of what he called 'the Nannies'. There would be no organising clubs, no rules, no official acceptances, no entrance fee, no race numbers, no official finishing order, and so on. Skippers would sail individual matches against each other, based on their own informal handicapping. More importantly, each skipper would take full personal responsibility for his or her own wellbeing, as on an independent passage. No rescue operations would be mounted, and any skipper unable to make land under his or her own efforts would be expected 'to die with dignity'. How refreshing!

The Series Two race was never run, and the OSTAR continued. The original organiser at the UK end, the Royal Western Yacht Club, largely ceded control to commercial interests. The final straw, as far as the origins of the race were concerned, came with the disbarring of yachts under thirty feet. *Jester* herself, or at least her reincarnation, the original having been lost at sea, was now disenfranchised from the race her owner had pioneered.

Ewen Southby-Tailyour perceived that, in this age where nannydom in every walk of life has reached an art form, the moment was ripe to resurrect Hasler's Series Two ideas and make them a reality. The concept was promoted exactly as per Hasler's outline, except for one major difference. This would now be a race for boats *under* thirty feet. The smaller boats, which were by far the majority in the early OSTARs, would have their race returned to them. With no rules or inspections, the emphasis would be firmly on individual skipper responsibility. Good seamanship would prevail over the win-at-all-costs mentality. Modest boats, on even more modest budgets, could once more find a place in the otherwise chequebook-dominated ocean racing circuit.

Ewen's perception was proven correct. Once announced, the Jester Challenge sparked huge interest and a large number of enquiries from prospective entrants. It felt like an idea whose time had come. This was for the ordinary yachtsman or yachtswoman who wanted a bigger personal challenge, but on a financially manageable scale. Scores of enquiries came in. This translated to sixteen confirmed entrants. There were the inevitable last minute withdrawals, including three from yachts already on their way to Plymouth.

By the time *Mingming* arrived at Plymouth, four days before the start, there were ten yachts still, as it were, in the race. This was twice as many as for the first OSTAR, so perhaps augurs well for the future. As I write this, there are already over sixty confirmed entrants for the next transatlantic Jester Challenge in 2010.

The most important participant in the first Jester Challenge was of course *Jester* herself. After an illustrious career under the command of that intrepid navigator Mike Richey, *Jester* had passed to Trevor Leek, himself a highly experienced small-boat ocean racer. We had hardly got *Mingming* tied alongside in Plymouth when the news was relayed that *Jester* had been dismasted in the Solent shortly after leaving for Plymouth. Oh no! We simply could not start the race without her. She was the physical embodiment of all it stood for. On the other hand the longer the race start was delayed, the closer came the hurricane season. A big effort was underway to get her to the start line on time. Collars, the mast makers, and constructors of the mast that had broken, were pulling out all the stops to build a new mast in time for the race. *Jester* herself was to be brought to

Plymouth by road. Hopefully she and the new mast would be united by midday on Saturday.

However, I still had an awful lot to do aboard *Mingming*. There was now not enough time to get back to London to pick up my stores and sort out last minute business affairs. Brenda and my son Sam would have to bring the stores down and help with the final preparations. After the quite horrible weather of the previous few weeks, we were graced with a run of perfect warm and sunny days in the lead-up to the start. A holiday atmosphere prevailed at the marina visitors' pontoon, where the contestants were moored alongside two deep. Most of us had already met earlier in the year at the London Boat Show, so friendships were quickly renewed and carried forward.

I was struck by the uncanny similarities with the 1974 trans-Tasman race. Once again there were ten competitors. Again, with the single exception of the Figaro One *Sterenn*, sailed by the charming Frenchman Eric Andlauer, there were no full-blown ocean-racing yachts. As with the earlier race, the skippers were united by their zealously guarded amateur – in the true sense of the word – status. There was nothing 'amateurish', however, about each skipper's preparation. There was a wealth of sea-going experience assembled there quietly beside the dock, not least Pete Hill of *Badger* fame, ex-naval officer Tony Head, and Sherman Wright, veteran of several transatlantic races. As with the trans-Tasman race I was at the small-boat end of the spectrum. On the other hand, time had caught up. I was no longer the youngest competitor. In fact I have to admit that I was now amongst the oldest.

6

Despite the light breeze I scarcely heard the bang of Ewen's shotgun. I saw the puff of smoke, though, from the talcum powder-filled cartridge, as it drifted to leeward of Ewen's cutter *Black Velvet*. Anchored a mile to the west of the Plymouth Breakwater, she marked the western end of the starting line. Rafted alongside her was *Jester*. Aboard *Jester* Trevor Leek and his son-in-law Rory, advised by Mike Richey, were hastily sorting out her running rigging. Her new mast had been stepped that morning, and *Black Velvet* had towed her out to the starting line. It was a great relief for all of us. We wanted her there. She would start a few minutes late, but that didn't matter.

It was an idyllic early-summer's day, and Plymouth Sound was alive with yachts, sails glistening in the bright sunshine. The four junk-rigged yachts entered for the race were complemented by a mass of Chinese lugsails from the Junk Rig Association rally, timed to coincide with the race start. Spectator boats zoomed around. The big launch hired to give friends and family a view of the start dutifully did the rounds. Conditions were perfect for photographs, except that in the light breeze the yachts were not really showing their paces to best advantage.

How many times had I tried to envisage this moment over the previous year? Myriad scenarios had played through my head, usually involving grey seas and a nasty blow from the south-west. In my mind's eye, I had seen us pounding seawards on starboard tack, a panel or two of the mainsail down, and myself snug inside with my head poking through the hatch. Here was now the reality; I was steering on deck, the self-steering servo pendulum still raised, my orange light weather jib set, and the fleet beating slowly out towards the glittering horizon in a warm and gentle west-south-westerly zephyr. It felt like a Sunday afternoon sail, not the start of an attempt on the north Atlantic. I found myself sailing parallel with Bill Churchouse in his Westerly 22 *Belgean*. We took photos of each other and had a final chat before slowly moving apart.

In tantalising light airs we worked our way out to sea. It was after six in the evening before we had passed the Eddystone lighthouse and its surrounding rocks. The fleet was already well separated. Only Mike Winter in *Jacinta*, a Cheverton 26, was properly in sight, ahead but to leeward. The rest had chosen to take a more inshore route. Later that evening the wind mercifully veered to north-west. For the first time in weeks we could sail with the sheets eased. All night it blew gently from that quarter.

As dawn broke I could make out the distinctive tan junk sail of Pete Hill's Kingfisher 20 *Shanti*, about a mile ahead. *Shanti*, along with Bill Churchouse's Westerly 22 *Belgean*, was probably the most closely matched boat to *Mingming*. In fact the three of us had made a wager, along the lines of the famous but apocryphal Hasler/Chichester half crown bet on the first transatlantic race. We had each put a pound in the kitty – winner takes all! With so much money riding on the outcome, the sight of *Shanti's* mainsail taunting me from ahead was the perfect stimulus to extract the best performance out of *Mingming*. By mid afternoon, with the Lizard now bearing slightly east of north, and the wind freshening heartily from the north-west, we had halved his lead.

Our cat-and-mouse duel continued all night. At one point we were just a couple of hundred yards apart, and by dawn the next day *Shanti* was lying half a mile astern on our port quarter. The wind continued to veer, to north-east – an ideal wind for gaining a quick offing. It was a hot wind too. I made a duck canvas cover for the main hatch to give some protection from the sun. *Shanti* was evidently taking a slightly more southerly course and by midday was almost hull down to the south-east.

I was disappointed with our noon position. Over the previous twenty-four hours we had made good just sixty nautical miles. I had expected this to be more. We still had a hundred miles to go to clear the two-hundred-metre depth contour and move properly off soundings.

For an hour that afternoon I was entertained by a particularly inquisitive fulmar. He – I'll call him a he as his close inspection of our rig suggested nerdy maleness – landed about twenty metres in front of the bow. As we sailed past he watched us intently, cocking his head to observe our strange mainsail with its orange and black insignia. Once we had left him well behind he took off and flew past to land once again in front of us, repeating the cycle. Round and round he went, over and over, seemingly fascinated. He was a pretty sight, with his well-set head and soft dark eye.

I was now having to scan the horizon with my binoculars to pick up *Shanti's* mainsail, now just a tiny dark spot on the horizon. By six that evening she was gone. For the first time since leaving Plymouth no vessels were in sight.

I felt liberated. At last we were on our own. The land was gone. We now had space, sea room, infinite possibility. Once more there was just the sky and the endlessly encircling horizon. Every last distraction from the pure business of sailing this simple little craft had edged away. We were back to the way I like it, to the *reductio ad absurdum* of little more than one tiny hull, a modest sail, some food and some water, alone but for the revolving sky above, and below, the black depths of the indifferent ocean.

7

What is it about, this attraction to the small boat, this obsession with making long sea passages the hard way, on a short
waterline length? I have spoken to many sailors about it, in
many cases trying to explain it, to overcome their increduli-
ty, their bafflement, at why, for me and others like me, it's
the only way we ever really want to go to sea.

Of course for me the origins lay ostensibly in the
Endeavour II shipwreck, that turned me against big craft and
too much reliance on other crewmembers. However the
decision that from then on I would sail single-handed in an
easily manageable boat by no means meant that it would
have to be in yachts of the size of *Roc* or *Mingming*. A thir-
ty-footer, even a properly rigged and laid out thirty-five
footer, could be sailed almost as easily, and would be considerably faster and more comfortable. Why would anyone wilfully want to forgo the opportunity of quicker, less physically demanding passages?

When I decided to build *Roc*, the question of cost was
certainly an element in the process. The cost of building and
maintaining a boat goes up by something like the square of
the increase in overall length. There is no doubt that many
ocean crossings have been made in small yachts simply
because the owner could not afford anything bigger.
However there is much, much more to it than that. When I

bought *Mingming* for, in ocean yachting terms, a paltry sum, I was in a position where I could comfortably have bought a boat costing twenty or thirty times as much. I could have bought a well-found ocean cruiser, a Victoria 30, for instance, with all the gear, all the bells and whistles that these days are considered obligatory even for a Sunday sail up the river. I could have, and I didn't. Why on earth not?

My personal taste is for sea-going that is a genuinely difficult challenge. This is based simply on the fact that the personal satisfaction derived from any achievement is in direct proportion to the difficulty of the task in hand. If you walk fifty yards to the corner shop to buy a newspaper, you are unlikely, unless for some reason you cannot walk easily, to get home bathed in the glow of having achieved something monumental. If, on the other hand, you spend a day climbing Helvellin by way of Striding Edge, you probably feel pretty pleased with yourself as you down a pint in a Cumbrian hostelry. If you were to spend days struggling on foot to cross a snow- and ice-covered uninhabited arctic island – I'm thinking here of H.W.Tilman's traverse of Bylot Island in the Canadian north, then you would have registered an experience that not only gives stupendous levels of personal satisfaction, but also changes for the better your view of yourself and of the gamut of possibility in life. The small-boat sailor generally has it tougher, longer and less comfortably than his larger-boat counterpart. But he, or she, earns his reward, by way of an immeasurably higher sense of achievement.

And yet that is by no means the whole story. Why do so many small-boat sailors, at the same time, eschew most of the paraphernalia of modern yachting? For myself the answer is straightforward: I want as few obstructions as possible lying between myself and the simple activity of sailing a yacht over the water. I don't want to be told what's going on by digital displays set up inside the yacht, fed by electronic sensors and radio signals from heaven knows where. Even more, I don't want to develop a dependency on these so-called 'aids'.

I want to use and develop my own senses. I want to feel everything that is going on directly, physically, viscerally, not via the intermediation of wires and computer chips. I want the experience to be as uncomplicated, and therefore as fundamental, as I can make it. I still want to live and relive those moments of myself as the ten-year-old, naively yearning to follow the big ships in a simple little dinghy. I want every single yard I cover to be won, hard-won if necessary, against whatever tide, winds or currents may from time to time oppose me, by the sole and patient use of whatever pure sailing skill or guile I have accrued.

Perhaps too, I want to share as best I can the experience of the great pioneers of sail. I want as far as is possible to create the conditions whereby our shrinking world can still feel immense, the oceans endless. This is why, for instance, I don't carry communication facilities. Being incommunicado for long, long periods was a basic feature of seagoing. I personally don't want to banalise the experience with, say, a satellite telephone, enabling me to have a daily chat with the folks back home. Going to sea single-handed is, to an extent, about coping with solitude and loneliness. However hard it may be, I would not want to water down that particular challenge.

The simpler and purer the experience, the more rewarding and satisfying I find it. Both *Roc* and *Mingming* were as basic as I could make them. *Roc* had no engine and no electrical equipment of any sort whatsoever, and of course in those pre-GPS days, all navigation was celestial. With *Mingming* I made two concessions as regards technology. The first, the best LED navigation lights available, were a response to the fact that this time much of my sailing would be in crowded waters. *Roc* had no lights, but was not required by international law to carry them, and was sailed mostly in areas almost totally devoid of shipping. On *Roc* I carried a powerful torch to shine on the mainsail if need be. I only ever had to do this once. On *Mingming* I needed the highest possible visibility at night.

I also carried a small hand-held GPS. This was principally as an aid to coastal pilotage. Navigating up and down the English Channel these days must be done in a very narrow – from the perspective of the engine-less single-hander – band between the coast and the northerly shipping lane. Sea room is simply not available. The ability to obtain an accurate fix, at night or, more particularly, in fog or very overcast conditions, goes a long way towards counterbalancing this very real constraint.

There are other fundamental reasons why I prefer simplicity. Simple, strong gear does not often break down. If it does fail, it is usually easily repaired with simple tools and basic materials. It is amazingly reassuring to put to sea knowing that you have no reliance whatsoever on the continuing functioning of complex electronic or mechanical systems. It removes a whole layer of potential anxiety. Nothing you can't fix easily can go wrong. You will always be in control.

The marine industry pulls yachtsmen further and further in the opposite direction, devising ever more expensive and sophisticated must-haves. It takes self-discipline not to be drawn in by the relentless marketing. The basic requirements for crossing an ocean under sail are no more than they always have been – a strong hull; a simple, easily managed rig; a good steering system with back-up; the ability to repair or rebuild anything on board while still at sea. It really isn't that complicated.

And one more point, before we press on with our story.

There are serious ecological considerations about which every leisure sailor should think seriously. Where is our poor beleaguered planet going to find the resources to fit out like Donald Trump apartments the burgeoning millions of over-sized leisure craft world-wide? The move towards ever bigger and more sophisticated yachts is a selfish and profligate waste for which future generations will curse us.

We know that climate change, driven by excessive carbon emissions, is destroying the polar icecaps. This is leading, amongst other things, to changes in oceanic salinity, acidity and temperature which will have fundamental effects on the ecology of the seas. Sea levels are set to rise alarmingly. Those of us who use the oceans for our pleasure should be the last to contribute wilfully to this destruction.

Sadly this is not the case. The average cruising or ocean racing yacht, even one that sails most of the time, still has to run its engines, or a separate generator, daily to charge the batteries that power cabin lights and navigation lights and fridges and heating systems and air-conditioning systems and showers and toilets and radar systems and GPS systems and stereo systems and auto-pilots and satellite 'phones and on-board computers and winches and windlasses and bilge pumps and AIS systems and bow thrusters and so on and so on ad infinitum. The long-term end result is that we will destroy what we purport to love. It is crazy. The simple yacht is a sustainable yacht, for all time.

8

So as *Shanti's* sail dipped below the horizon, consigning us to an empty ocean, I felt, for the first time since slipping our mooring at Burnham-on-Crouch almost two months previously, that we had at last reached our proper environment. This was the habitat for which *Mingming* had been prepared. The wind was freshening from east-north-east, with Force 6 to 7 forecast. I was looking forward to a fast downwind run over the Little Sole Bank and off the continental shelf into the real waters of the Atlantic. With a following wind I did not need a headsail. Both my little jibs were now well lashed down on the fore-deck. I hoped that from here on I could sail on the mainsail alone, handling it from the main hatch, with no need to go on deck.

I was already starting to enjoy and appreciate what I called in my log the '*Jester* principle': the concept of ocean sailing from the inside of the vessel, with no requirement ever to leave the warmth and safety of the cabin. I did not yet have *Mingming* to a state of total perfection as regards this principle, as will be seen later, but it was by now very close. I recalled the story of the contrast between the arrivals of Francis Chichester and 'Blondie' Hasler at New York at the end of the first transatlantic race. Chichester had worked tirelessly throughout the crossing, constantly on deck changing headsails, reefing and unreefing his sizeable mainsail. He arrived in a state of near exhaustion. Hasler, who seemed to have spent most of his time practising his ukulele-banjo and sampling the various wines he had on board, arrived in cardigan and carpet slippers, more rested than when he had left Plymouth.

As the wind increased throughout the night and I dropped, one by one, four panels of the sail, each manoeuvre requiring just a few seconds standing in the hatch, I started to fully appreciate how well suited the junk rig was for this kind of sailing. I had infinite control of the sail, down to the last few inches, but could exercise that control without ever having to struggle into oilskins and a harness and risk the dangers of the deck. I was already starting to become addicted to the safe haven of the cabin.

Running downwind, *Mingming* was so calm and sedate, so quiet, that at one point that night I had to open the hatch and look out to check that she was in fact moving. She was making four knots or so, but stretched on my bunk below in a warm sleeping bag I had no impression of forward movement. *Mingming* was always very stable downwind, even in big seas. I suspect that the twin keels, with their high ballast ratio, discouraged the pendulum rolling that a deep single keel can often create.

By noon the next day, after a day's run of ninety-five miles, we were crossing the two-hundred-metre depth contour, under a single panel of the sail, still running before what was now a half gale. The sky was a clear brilliant blue, with an insistent sun flooding the cabin with crisp brightness. Running out into the Atlantic in this building following sea, the swells seemed to lose some of their steepness as the waves lengthened to an easier oceanic lope. I had managed to set up a good balance between the size and set of the mainsail, the wind vane angle, and the chain linkage to the tiller. *Mingming* ran on easily, with just the slightest tiller movements to keep her on course. The Corribee is extremely light on the helm in most conditions, but I wanted always to minimise any strain on the steering system. Although I was better prepared for a loss of steering than I had been on *Roc*, I was intent on nursing *Mingming* carefully through any heavy weather.

That night, perhaps because I was now more relaxed as we moved away from land and shipping, I fell into a deeper sleep than normal and slept through my thirty minute alarm. I woke at two in the morning after three and a half hours of uninterrupted slumber. I felt much better for a good sleep, but resolved not to let it happen again. The weather held without change, except for yet another slight increase in wind strength and, when daylight came, noticeably later as we made our southing, a hazier look to the unclouded sky. I had hoped to notch up a day's run of over a hundred miles, but was disappointed when our noon position showed we had once again only covered just over ninety miles.

I raised a panel in an attempt to crank up our speed a little, but within an hour had put things back the way they were. The extra panel certainly gave more speed, but our steady course-making was lost as we rounded up in the stronger gusts before the self-steering gear could make the necessary corrections. I really did not like this sort of nervy, erratic progress, nor the additional strain it was putting on the steering gear as the servo pendulum dragged us back on course.

I settled us back to the lovely balance and smooth ride we had enjoyed all night under a single panel. Apart from the relaxed and unstressful progress this gave, there was something very reassuring about the inherent strength of the rig in this configuration. As I had written in my log that morning:

This junk rig is a marvel for fine adjustments, and the last panel, supported by the yard at the head, the sail bundle at the foot, and two lazyjacks on the lee side, is under no strain whatsoever. With the forward pressure of the sail just a few feet above the mast partners, the mast is rock solid in heavy weather.

9

We were sailing well, *Mingming* was bone dry inside and I was able to spend most of my time stretched out on my bunk resting, occasionally dozing off for a brief spell, or just thinking. I had deliberately not brought along any books to read. I wanted to keep my focus on the here and now, to live every moment of this voyage with my mind right there on *Mingming*, not transported off to some other imaginary world.

Long-distance sailors often love reading, especially fiction. It takes them away, temporarily, from the stress and monotony of small-boat confinement. I had decided that, if I were once again going off adventuring to sea, it would be odd, if not downright illogical, to then want to read fictional adventures in order to escape my own real one. If time passed slowly as a result, if I got bored, then so be it. I would just have to learn to cope with it. It was, like loneliness, fear and fatigue, a potential part of the package.

I took lots of writing material though: waterproof pens and big notebooks. I wrote a comprehensive log. My plan was to circumvent potential boredom by intense observation. I would observe and record, observe and record. I would try to live every privileged moment to the full. Apart from my short periods of sleep, I would never switch off mentally. I would harvest the fullest experience I could from my time at sea.

However all was not well. I had very little appetite. Nothing in my stores, preserved or fresh, really appealed, apart from the occasional crisp green granny smith apple. I was almost forcing myself to eat my usual three meals a day. I could not work out what was the problem. I was not nauseous. I had not experienced any seasickness. I just lacked appetite, and was unusually lethargic. I had now been at sea for nearly a week – much longer than I would normally need to find my sea legs. It was a nuisance, and disappointing. I put it down to some sort of low-grade *mal de mer*. Blame the French...

The wind eased down to a comfortable Force 4 to 5, and veered slowly round to the south-east. The swells, which, measured as best I could off the top of my wind vane, had reached about eight feet, smoothed out somewhat. Before too long we had the full mainsail set again and were going along quite nicely, shy reaching on port tack. Our course since taking our departure from the Lizard had held steady at about two-forty magnetic.

I had spent months researching and thinking about what route to take to Newport. Finally, and perhaps spurred on by the lousy weather we had suffered coming down Channel in May, which had made the thought of some warmth and sunshine somehow rather appealing, I had settled on the more southerly Azores route. We were therefore heading for a point approximately 40N 35W, to the north-west of the Azores. From there we would curve west and perhaps slightly more south, across a great oceanic no-man's land, before curving back up to the north-west for the final approach to Newport.

Friday 9th June dawned in thick fog, which hung there all morning, despite the best efforts of a watery sun to burn it off. It was cold too, under the grey mantle. For once, we were not the only sailing craft on the steely Atlantic surface.

There were sails as far as the eye could see in every direction, thousands, hundreds of thousands, millions, every one glinting in the weak light. We plunged along through them for hour after hour, pushing them boldly aside with our bow wave. Jack sail-by-the-winds, *velella velella*, were holding an offshore regatta. These tiny jellyfish, with a round float supporting a rigid and transparent curved sail, about two inches long and an inch high, covered every square metre of the ocean. They became our constant companions for the next few weeks.

We were evidently moving into some new area of pelagic habitat, for as well as the great fleets of jack sail-by-the-winds, we started to meet colonies of buoy barnacles, *dosima fascicularis,* floating on, or just under, the surface. A spongy sphere, about the size of a tennis ball, provided the home-built flotation for the twenty or more barnacles that grew out of it, sprouting their thick muscular stalks in every direction from the central float.

That afternoon, by which time the fog had finally lifted to leave a vivid blue sky, I managed to fish out, with my hand, one of these heavy balls of barnacles. The body of each barnacle was protected by an almost translucent bivalve shell. Through the narrow crack between the lips of each half protruded scores of leg-like feelers. I made a rough sketch then returned the buoy barnacle condominium to the water. These floating colonies accompanied us for the next few weeks, in huge numbers too. Unlike the jack sail-by-the-winds, though, they rarely seemed to be randomly scattered over the surface. Almost without fail they formed themselves into perfectly straight lines to windward. I could only guess that they secreted something into the water that signalled to the next one down the line where to hold its position.

Despite the brilliant weather the barometer was falling, and the shipping forecast, which I could just pick up very faintly, was predicting gales for north-west FitzRoy. Throughout the night I gradually reefed *Mingming* down as the wind got up from the south. By six the next morning we were in the top end of a Force 7, with gale force gusts. I dropped the sail completely and lashed the bundle firmly together. I took off the wind vane and stowed it below. I had a spare, but had seen on *Roc* what a breaking wave could do to a self-steering gear, and this time would take no chances. I lashed the tiller amidships with shock-cord, to reduce contrary stresses between the rudder and the tiller lashings.

By seven the near gale had gone round to the west, so I tacked ship to lay-to on starboard tack. The waves were getting up, perhaps to twelve feet or so, rolling in steeply from the west, but there was nothing threatening about them. *Mingming*, light, buoyant and seemingly quite at ease, rose to them effortlessly.

In my log I summed up the midday weather forecast in one word:

Horrible!

A severe low-pressure system was now a hundred miles west of FitzRoy. Force 9 winds were expected. Fortunately we were by now well into the southern part of the FitzRoy area, so should escape the worst. The Jester Challengers who had chosen to take a more direct route west were not so lucky. On that same day they were hit by two closely-spaced depressions with winds up to Force 10.

Although 'weather routeing' in most yachts, apart from the fastest racers, is not really viable, I was nevertheless impelled to set some sail and run off to the south. It would make little difference, given the speed at which these systems advance, but taking some form of evasive action, whether effective or not, would at least make me feel better. We ran to the south-south-east under one panel.

Sure enough the wind gradually eased and by ten that

evening was down to Force 5, now from south-south-west. On we plunged with three panels raised. With the barometer once more rising and the depression gone off to harry unfortunate sailors in the English Channel, I tacked to sail west. This put us head on into the big seas left over from the storm. Poor old *Mingming*, close-hauled on her weakest point of sailing, could not develop enough drive to power through them. We resumed our previous heading, moving more comfortably through a night so cold that in the cabin I was plagued by an annoying outbreak of wintry condensation.

10

I was still troubled by lack of appetite. The evening meal of rice and tuna that I cooked for myself stretched out to become my breakfast and even part of my lunch. Another little dark cloud was slowly forming in the back of my mind. Despite the recent storm we had generally had very favourable conditions so far, with winds from the north. However we seemed to be settling into an average daily distance made good of just over sixty miles. A two and a half knot average speed for a tiny, junk-rigged yacht in oceanic conditions with a contrary current was maybe not too bad, but I had been counting on slightly more. My calculations for the crossing had been predicated on an average speed over the ground of three knots, giving a daily distance of just under seventy-five nautical miles. Allowing for all the extra miles that must inevitably be sailed in a predominantly upwind crossing, this would translate to between forty-five and sixty days at sea. On that basis we would arrive at Newport sometime during the second half of July. This would already be uncomfortably close to the height of the hurricane season, but was just tolerable.

My current average daily distance was starting to suggest a potential crossing time of more like fifty-five to seventy days. There would be nothing unusual about this. In the first transatlantic race Val Howells, sailing his folkboat *Eira*, took sixty-three days. Jean Lacombe in *Cap Horn* took seventy-four days. Both of these times were on the southern route I was taking. I had provisioned *Mingming* for one hundred days, in case of damage.

The problem was that hurricanes are more frequent and more severe than forty years ago. All the Jester Challenge skippers had been given the 2006 hurricane forecast from the US Meteorological Service. Its main conclusion was that the season would be almost as severe as the devastating 2005 season. A seventy-day crossing would push our arrival well into August. My Imray-Iolaire North Atlantic Ocean Passage Chart was succinct on the matter. No weather data was given for August or September. Instead it said simply: *Boats should not be sailing as the Atlantic hurricane frequency is too high...* Well, I would just carry on for the time being and see how things went.

By the 12th of June, our ninth day at sea, the wind had swung back to the north – a light north-north-westerly in this case. The seas were flattening, though still a bit lumpy in the leftover slop. For the first time in several days we could set a direct course for our mid-Atlantic target. I raised the small jib to give us a bit more push. It was an idyllic, much warmer day, with cotton-wool clouds moving sedately across a deep-blue sky.

I had by now stopped taking celestial sights. Prior to setting sail I had stupidly forgotten to check the index error on my Ebbco sextant. The error was now about 16 minutes of arc – over five times the Admiralty recommended maximum. To correct it meant adjusting the springs holding the mirrors with a tiny Allen key. This was difficult enough on land, as the turning of the minuscule screws required the touch and precision of a watchmaker. I knew it would be impossible to adjust the sextant properly at sea. I was therefore navigating on a single noon position each day from my hand-held GPS.

In the very light airs we had made good just fifty nautical miles over the previous twenty-four hours.

A near disaster was averted that afternoon when I went aft to make an adjustment to the self-steering gear. By pure chance I noticed that the machine screw that secures the linkage between the wind vane and the servo-pendulum had worked itself loose and was just about to fall out. If it had dropped into the sea I'm not at all sure that I could have kept the steering gear working.

As the day progressed a more purposeful breeze got up, slowly veering to the north. For the first time we were making our course with a strong beam wind and a building sea. *Mingming* rolled heavily as each steep swell passed under her. For the first time she was taking the occasional hefty thump on the side. From time to time a wave top curled over the side deck to fill the small cockpit.

The wind veered further towards the north-east, increasing to a half gale and setting up a nasty cross-sea against the heavy swells still rolling in from the north west. I was starting to appreciate the reassurance that comes with sailing an unsinkable yacht. *Mingming* was taking her worst battering so far, but, despite the heavy blows jarring her once in a while, I felt quite at ease. We were by now broad reaching, with just one panel set, through a confused sea. *Mingming* felt tight and inflexible. My sense was that the new forward bulkhead in particular, and the foam jammed in tightly between the stem and the deck forward of that bulkhead, eliminated any flexing in the front half of the boat. The alterations aft had turned her into a little fortress.

11

I felt confident that *Mingming* could weather any storm the eastern Atlantic could throw at her. However a difficult debate was still under way somewhere in the back of my mind. The question was simply this – *was I prepared to sail Mingming into the north-western Atlantic at the height of the hurricane season?* It was by now quite clear that only exceptionally benign conditions could get us to Newport before the end of July. Weighing on me was Mike Richey's comment about the Azores route I was taking – that one could have a thousand miles of light headwinds for the last leg.

In my mind's eye I saw the Jester Challenge fleet strung out across the Atlantic, the mighty *Sterenn* at the head, the rest forming a growing ungainly line, with *Mingming* patiently plugging along in the rear. The scene played on: *One by one they arrive at Newport, scrambling in before the bad weather hits. One yacht is still out there, one of the smallest of the fleet...A hurricane sweeps up from the south. Another Katrina. No, worse than that... Nothing is heard ever again.........* and so on and so on. I realised that what was concerning me, as much as the reasonable desire not to get caught out in a full-blown hurricane, was fear of somehow marring the success of this first Jester Challenge. The event had, inevitably, thrown up the usual raft of detractors and nay-sayers. It was very important, perhaps vital to the continuation of the idea, that all the competitors should make port safely and under their own steam, so to speak.

I debated the issue with myself, day after day, batting the arguments from one side of my head to the other. Time after time I pulled out the passage chart and made endless calculations and what-if projections, walking my dividers back and forth over the chart. I just did not know what to do. To turn round and head back north, thereby throwing in the towel on the Challenge, went against every fibre in my body. Giving up was not in my vocabulary. On the other hand, any hard-nosed, perhaps pessimistic but to my mind therefore more realistic, assessments of my likely crossing time put us well into the danger zone.

What to do? What to do? With a beam wind we had just clocked a day's run of a fraction over a hundred miles. A few weeks like that would quickly break the back of the crossing, put us well ahead of our schedule. As I ate my way through the stores, and drank my water, we would get lighter and, presumably, faster. On the other hand, my mind-set as a sailor is naturally defensive. Perhaps sailing so much without an engine encourages the habit of always building in large margins of error, of always assuming the worst will happen and constructing a strategy from that starting point. My instinct was not to hope blindly for an unlikely run of exceptional daily distances, but rather the opposite, to assume every kind of adversity, and then see where that would leave us. Maybe I was just getting more cautious in my old age. I certainly valued survival as an objective.

My appetite was improving slowly, but I was by now having to cope with my usual second-week miseries. Indecision gnawed away at me. *What to do? What to do?* I tried to dissect all my motivations, hoping that a rigorous analysis may help me see the dilemma more clearly. Did I want or need to prove anything to myself? Not really, not any more. I knew now too beyond doubt that *Mingming* was an excellent little sea boat. Did I want or need to prove anything to anyone else? Well, I would dearly love to complete the crossing to show the detractors that *Mingming* was capable of it. On the other hand, to carry on wilfully into a hurricane area, with potentially disastrous consequences, would play into the hands of the nannies and rule freaks. It was important that they should have no ammunition to play with. From that perspective, to carry on was a high-risk strategy – something of a win-all or lose-all.

Was I concerned about the good name of the Jester Challenge? Absolutely. There had been more interest and publicity about the event than I would have imagined. It was now very much in the public domain. It was vital this first Challenge should pass off without incident. An ignoble but prudent retreat was no doubt a better option than deliberately courting excessive danger. Was I concerned about my own safety? Yes, but I had every confidence in *Mingming*. In purely personal terms I was not unduly worried about meeting a hurricane. I felt that *Mingming* would hang together and remain afloat. The biggest potential danger was of being rolled and dismasted. I was prepared for that. Why not just carry on and to hell with the consequences?

Round and round the arguments went, while we ran on before the north-easterly half gale. The longer I delayed a decision the closer we got to some sort of no-man's-land, when sailing back would be almost as unpalatable as entering the hurricane zone. I was by now a few hundred miles to the north east of the Azores. I pulled out my Azores chart and updated it with the corrections' sheet, just in case I needed it. I thought about altering course to the south and calling in there, but finally rejected the idea. I didn't have the correct papers and was not sure whether that would cause difficulties or not. But anyway what was the point? I was embarked on an ocean voyage, not a holiday cruise.

Fourteen days out from Plymouth, with mixed feelings, and, appropriately, suffering indigestion from some tinned squid I had eaten, I brought *Mingming* round, hard on the wind, to start the long haul back to Burnham-on-Crouch. Prudence had won the day, by a very small margin. I would, after all, play it safe. The priority was to arrive in port, wherever that may be, without incident. I was extremely well provisioned, and had virtually as much time as I liked to retrace my track back to the Essex coast.

My Jester Challenge was, for this time anyway, over. However the voyage was still very much alive. I set myself a new challenge to help me retain my focus and resolve – the Mingming Challenge. I would, if I could, sail *Mingming* back from this spot out in the north Atlantic to her Royal Corinthian Yacht Club mooring at Burnham-on-Crouch, without going ashore, and stopping only if absolutely necessary to shelter or to sleep on the difficult last coastal leg. I would, despite pulling out of the main challenge, nonetheless do my best to complete a significant little voyage, challenging in its own way. I would get us home the hard way, in one non-stop leg through the western approaches, up Channel, round the South Foreland, across the Thames Estuary and home to Burnham. Even then I knew that would be tough to do. I had no idea, though, just how much this second half of the voyage would test my patience and endurance.

12

Fortunately my indigestion cleared up quickly. I felt better, too, for having made a decision. Even today, I don't really know whether it was the correct decision or not, but it was made, I was committed, and I had to bend my will to the next phase of the voyage and get on with it.

By dawn of the 17th June the wind had backed to north-north-west, easing to about Force 5. For a few hours we were able to lay our proper course for the Lizard, about nine hundred miles away, on about fifty degrees magnetic, going along nicely under full mainsail. My morale lifted as we settled in to the new task. The leading wind did not last long, coming back to due north and heading us to a more easterly course. By afternoon the wind had gone back to north-east and dropped right away. We were going nowhere, and that in the wrong direction. It was frustrating, but I could not imagine these northerly winds lasting too much longer. We would surely pick up a south-westerly before long. We did indeed pick up a south-westerly – a mere eighteen days later, by which time we were south of Portland Bill.

However the wind strengthened and for three days or so it blew relatively consistently and strongly from the north-west, sometimes with more north in it, sometimes more west. We plunged along doggedly into it, occasionally with the sheets eased slightly, but often as not close-hauled. The weather was mostly grey and overcast, with frequent bouts of misty light rain. The sea was once again lumpy and often uncomfortable, with the predominant swells, still from the north-west, fighting it out with a lesser contender from the south-west. But progress was good. We were now averaging over seventy miles a day to windward. Of course the Gulf Stream had switched from foe to friend. Having that great broad current under us made an inevitable difference to our daily runs. It was now adding twelve miles or so to our daily performance, rather than subtracting them.

On the morning of 22nd June, our twentieth day at sea, conditions changed. The wind dropped, came up a bit, dropped some more, swung round to the north-east, dropped some more, came up a bit, then dropped with a faint splash into the ocean and, for the rest of that day, hid resolutely beneath the surface. By early afternoon we were totally, utterly becalmed. There was nor breath nor very much motion:

Alone, alone, all, all alone
Alone on a wide, wide sea!
Unless this wind picks up damn soon
We won't be home for tea...

We lay with the sails hanging limply, slatting back and forth in the leftover swell. I sat in the cockpit, happy to be on deck in this calm weather, and, for the first time on the voyage, hung over the low gunwale and watched for hour after hour the infinite procession of marine creatures drifting slowly past in the clear blue pelagic water. Foremost amongst these, in both size and numbers, were the salps, *salpa cylindrica*.

At first you could mistake a salp for a strangely shaped jellyfish, with its tubular gelatinous body. It moves gently along by pumping water through itself, extracting its meal of plankton as it goes. Like the jack sail-by-the-winds we had encountered previously, they were there literally in their millions. It was not possible, for a week or so, to look over the side in calm conditions and not see scores of them making their silent, eerie way just below the surface.

Sometimes they were single animals, eight or nine inches long; others were joined up in small groups, five or six, identically-sized, connected together in symbiotic harmony. Most amazing were the great spiralling bandoleers of salps, sometimes hundreds to a spiral, often of tiny one inch baby salps, but from time to time great curving snakes of mature creatures, looking from above like some weird sea monster. Salps are one of the best-adapted and fastest growing multicellular animals. They have a small brain and a primitive nervous system. They may well yet inherit the earth.

We had entered a new phase of the voyage, one of calms and flukey winds, which lasted for the next ten days or so. With light and unpredictable winds shifting constantly between north-east and north-west, stopping for a short while at every gradation between the two, we settled into a twenty-four hour routine of incessant adjustment of the self-steering setting and of sail trim. My jibs were now hard at work again as we clawed slowly to windward, always close-hauled, only rarely on an ideal heading, shifting from one tack to the other as the insubstantial wind played out its unending gyrations.

The Atlantic took on a new character, with day after day of gentle undulation, the surface rising and falling to the faint respiration of the sleeping giant beneath. Glassy patches set up patterns across the faint cat's-paws stretching out to the horizon. Sometimes the emphasis reversed – the sea as pristine and polished as a royal table top, with just a hint of a darker line where the elusive breeze ruffled the mirrored surface, somewhere over there, away towards the edge of what was now our only world.

The sky abandoned its urgent wheeling. The procession of cloud forms slowed to a funereal shuffle, then stopped dead. The banks of cloud certainly moved and changed, but with such a slowly-evolving kaleidoscopic subtlety that it was impossible to be sure how or when they had changed, whence they came, where they were bound.

For hours at a time I sat in the main hatch and watched the sky, desperate for some clue to help unlock its inscrutability. Nothing ever came. No wind came, for longer than a few hours at a time. No cloud patterns that I could decipher hove into view. Day after day we lay under an inert and mysterious sky, catching the begrudging bounty it sent down from time to time – an hour of breeze from here, a half hour zephyr from there, a puff on this cheek, then one on the other, and always from somewhere ahead.

We were still out of range of the long wave BBC shipping forecast, so could not pick up any crumbs of comfort from there. It didn't matter anyway. We were locked in an inescapable here and now, so why worry? As each day passed and we played out once more our ceaseless game of cat-and-mouse with the fickle breeze, I grew more resigned to it, more philosophic, less agitated at the often painfully slow progress. As they always will, time and habituation worked their effect, imposing rhythm and acceptance on the daily round. This is the way it is, so learn to live with it.

My appetite was now fully restored. Now well into our third week at sea, I had broken through the loneliness barrier to reach that state of relaxed adaptation in which time, and that other place beyond the horizon, become immaterial. Put another way, I was now completely at home out there on *Mingming*, rolling gently to the almost imperceptible swell, hundreds of miles from land and the destructive madness of human aspiration. My tiny yacht, with its single narrow berth, a few shelves and lockers, a simple spirit stove, a plastic bucket for bodily needs, room to sit comfortably but not to stand; this little capsule, along with the supporting ocean stretching away to the curve of the horizon, was now a complete and self-sufficient world in itself.

13

My days had no beginning and no end, but seemed nonetheless to start at breakfast. This was usually eaten at about eight in the morning, and was always a bowl of Jordan's fruit muesli with milk. Along with that I usually had a mug of tea. Washing up was simply a matter of cleaning my plastic bowl and spoon with some kitchen roll. I don't like dish cloths on small boats. They get permanently damp and smelly. I always keep a big supply of strong kitchen roll on board. It serves for every cleaning job.

After breakfast was tidying up time, first myself, then the boat. It is tempting to let yourself go a bit at sea, particularly in the beard department. I usually shaved properly, with water – just a tiny drop, razor and all, every other day. It freshens you up wonderfully and adds a bit of zest to a sometimes crumpled spirit. On a long voyage with no laundry facilities there is obviously a limit as to how often you can change your clothes, but that too can be an invigorating treat. I never waste water to clean my teeth. Toothbrush and paste is all you need. Saliva and plenty of spitting overboard do the rest.

Overnight the cabin would often get a bit messy, with hats, blankets, sea boots, torches, pencils, dividers and the like strewn around. Once I had myself in order I attacked the cabin, putting everything back where it should be, rolling up and stowing my sleeping bag, blankets, sweaters. Everything back to square one for another daily round.

All this, except for the overboard spitting, was done sitting in my main central position on the sole starboard bunk. Behind, as a backrest, was the navigation locker with its fold-down door. Directly opposite on the port side was my table, used mainly for navigation and writing, that swung forward if necessary to reveal the little stove and galley space beneath. There was little in the boat, in the way of daily necessities, that could not be reached from this sitting position.

Feeling clean and fresh, in a shipshape cabin, I then, if necessary, wrote up my log. Keeping my log going is usually a continuous process. I write down everything as it happens, but sometimes, particularly overnight, I may get a bit behind. If there was no ship handling to do, and I was happy with my course and navigation, I then had the prospect of a morning to myself. If I had been up a lot during the night, I may have stretched out lazily on my bunk and taken it easy. Usually I preferred not to sleep again. I would get too dozy and lethargic. A short nap after lunch was OK, but as far as possible I avoided sleeping in the morning.

If the weather was fine I would often sit in the companionway, my eyes just above the hatch, and, mesmerized by the rhythm of our progress through the faint swells, observe the world around. Sometimes small flocks of Cory's shearwaters wheeled in to take a look. Once, bizarrely, a male peregrine falcon circled us several times then set off resolutely north, heading for Ireland. A little tern came and went. Several times great schools of dolphins passed us, leaping clear of the water to show off their prodigious musculature and athleticism. Always there was a small petrel or two in sight, dodging busily along close to the surface, searching intently for some oceanic holy grail, ignoring us completely.

In calm weather a faint scuffling on the surface heralded the passage of the little pelagic crab, *polybius henslowii*, Henslow's swimming crab. They were swimming gamely north, using their flattened claws as paddles. As the hull of *Mingming* loomed predatorially above them, they gave up their frantic scrabbling and sank down a foot or two into the protective gloom. Their progress across the surface was so painfully, pathetically slow, and yet so despairingly energetic, that *Mingming* seemed jet-propelled by comparison.

If conditions were not suitable for sitting in the hatchway, and if I felt creative, I stayed below and wrote. Usually what I wrote was nonsense. As on *Roc*, where tedious hours at the tiller were lightened by reams of comic invention, I gave often myself over to the concoction of humorous verse. To bring, say, a little limerick to a satisfying and hopefully amusing perfection can take hours of play and replay. A morning of intense verbal reflection may not yield any worthwhile result. Then again, it just may:

A navigator, with consummate care,
Took some sights at the Folies Bergeres.
With his sextant he observed that the world is quite curved
And the heavenly bodies are bare...

Well, it passed the time and kept me amused. I even started a *magnum opus*, a poetic saga entitled *The Odyssey of Mr & Mrs Newley-Richards: An Epic Tale of Modern Yachting*. It started thus:

Mr & Mrs Newley-Richards bought a Jeanneau at the Show
Thogh they'd seldom been near water, it seemed the
*   trendy way to go.*
Bought two sets of matching oilies, and a Breton cap for
*   him;*

For her a set of salty tea towels that matched the curtains down below.

I penned a letter to the editor of Yachting World, putting him right, I hope, on a few misconceptions about the smaller contestants in the Jester Challenge. It was eventually published, with not too many excisions.

14

As the morning passed, the midday ritual approached and I checked my watch more and more often. As I was not taking a meridian altitude, I had settled on twelve noon British Summer Time as my marker for a daily GPS fix and calculation of our daily run. As we once more started to pick up BBC long-wave, there was also the 1204 hours shipping forecast to note down. As midday approached I would start to get slightly nervous. By then I had usually made a guess at our likely distance made good over the previous twenty-four hours. Would we have done better than I had predicted, or would there once again be disappointment? Would the next cross on the chart move us substantially towards our goal, or would we be left mouldering close to the same spot as yesterday?

I got the little hand-held GPS out of its waterproof plastic container in the navigation locker, ready to be switched on and proffered to the sky, an offering to the new gods of push-button wizardry. My Roberts radio was retrieved from its shelf and unwrapped out of its various leather and plastic casings. A notebook and pencil were produced for recording our position and making any notes from the weather forecast. Everything was readied. My watch was consulted yet again. One minute to twelve. Time!

The GPS was switched on and dangled out of the after

port-light on the bridge-deck to seek out its satellites and work its black arts. Once it had a reading, I quickly noted it down. Now the radio was switched on. With luck the short news bulletin preceding the shipping forecast would be nearly over. Who cared who was killing whom today and with what self-righteous justifications? Of what relevance were the latest rancid evasions emanating from the mouths of the craven and the duplicitous, our great leaders? I just couldn't abide listening to all that stuff, having it stain and sully, with its blind, self-immolating solipsism, the great cycle of untarnished nature unfolding all around.

With the weather forecast noted, our noon position could then be marked on the passage chart and the distance made good from the previous day's position measured off. Invariably five minutes would then be spent playing with the dividers, measuring off just about every other distance I could think of. How far are we now from the Lizard? What's the distance made good over the last two days…three days…four days? How close are we to our outward track? How close is the nearest land? How far are we now from Bogota? How many days would it take to sail to Svalbard?

Having comprehensively re-established our location in space and time, the log could then be written up. In went our noon latitude and longitude, distance made good, barometer reading, current weather conditions, forecast weather conditions. I usually then reviewed the last twenty-four hours. How well or badly had we done in relation to expectations? What was the general mood aboard ship? What was now our likely time to the Lizard? Were we sailing the right course for the conditions and forecast? Anything else pertinent? Any other business? It was the Chairman's Report and Outlook, issued daily to a shareholder meeting of one.

Then lunch. As with breakfast, this rarely varied. For long single-handed voyages I think it's very important to maintain a stable eating regime, with not too many surprises or variations for the body to cope with. Find a good rhythm, the foods your body likes and processes efficiently, and stick to them. That way you'll establish a regular and healthy round of intake and evacuation. For lunch I ate a selection of rye bread, pumpernickel bread, sunflower seed bread and so on, mainly with butter and cheese and perhaps some jam or marmite. The rich dark breads, vacuum-packed, keep for months and months. Once again, lunch was quick and easy to make, with just a plastic plate and a knife to wipe afterwards. This was followed by fresh fruit, if I had any, or home-made fruit cake or flapjack. Drink was water, usually with lime juice added.

By the time lunch was over and everything, GPS and radio included, was wrapped up and restored to its rightful place, the surfaces wiped of crumbs and spills, and a second round of folding and tidying completed, it was well past one o'clock. The long afternoon now stretched out ahead. Often, after a careful all-round check for any shipping, I took a thirty-minute nap. During the early part of the return leg we rarely encountered any marine traffic. I saw nothing at all throughout one five-day spell. Nonetheless I kept a careful and regular watch, day and night. As we drew closer to the latitude of the north Spanish coast, the occasional merchant ship or fishing boat passed us, usually heading west or east.

It was easy enough to fall asleep in the warm afternoons. Down below I always wore loose, comfortable clothing and thick woollen socks. Everything possible was done to keep the ambience in the cabin warm, dry and relaxed. Sea boots were kept handy for going on deck, but in good conditions I could hop up on deck and back in my socks. Only *in extremis* would I be forced to don waterproofs.

In fine weather I often spent time on deck by choice, but I came to hate being forced to go on deck against my will.

This happened regularly throughout most days, and was mostly my own fault. Firstly the very simple remote control arrangement on the self-steering gear proved inadequate for ocean work. It was very difficult to set from the hatch and even if I did manage to adjust it accurately, it would not hold the vane in the right position for long. After a while I abandoned it and reverted to going aft myself to set and lock the vane in position.

A trip aft on deck in bad weather or heavy seas was not much fun. Sea boots, wet weather gear and harness had to be pulled on. The main hatch was opened and a harness clip attached to a strong point just aft of the cabin. I climbed out onto a heaving deck, quickly shutting the hatch behind me to keep the driving spray or rain out of the cabin. Already half soaked, cursing at having had to leave the tranquillity of my below-deck universe, I worked my way to the transom, often on my knees, transferring my harness clips from one strong point to the next. I adjusted the wind vane to the correct angle and locked it firmly in place, then started on the short but arduous journey back to warmth and safety.

My boots and waterproofs, now covered with rain or spray, or both, dribbled water everywhere, ruining the zealously-guarded dryness of the cabin. I pulled them off quickly and stowed them in their place in what was once the port quarter berth. All the water brought in was then mopped up with kitchen roll. I sat quietly for a minute or two, regaining my composure and settling once more to the peace of the cabin, then checked our heading on the internal compasses. Oh no! We're still ten degrees off course. The wind has hauled round slightly. There's nothing for it. We've got to repeat the whole damn performance yet again...

I really should have remembered from *Roc* how annoying and debilitating these frequent trips aft can become. To an extent I had, which was why I had fixed up a remote control arrangement in the first place. In retrospect, though, I should have paid a lot more attention to constructing a more robust and efficient system. This I have now done. However, there was a second irritating and totally foreseeable factor, it too concerned with the self-steering, that also necessitated innumerable sorties through the hatch.

Small adjustments to the boat's heading can be made simply by altering the steering line chain attachment to the tiller by a link or two, sometimes in combination with a mainsheet adjustment. This is particularly good for coping with very small wind shifts, and changes in wind strength that alter the balance of the yacht fractionally. But, however far I leaned out of the hatch, I could not quite manage to reach the chain and the link fitting on the tiller. They evaded my straining fingers by just a few tantalising centimetres. This was infuriating, as once again it meant I had to haul myself up on deck to make even the smallest adjustments.

It was even more infuriating because I knew well before leaving Plymouth that I couldn't reach the tiller chain from the hatch. It would have been a very quick and simple matter to make a longer tiller and change the steering line leads. At the time it didn't seem a priority and I overlooked it. Now I was daily, sometimes hourly, paying the price of a careless oversight. Needless to say, *Mingming* now has a longer tiller.

15

However, the afternoons were mostly calm and sunny during this period, so I was often on deck by choice. After my nap I would resume my study of the marine life that shared the ocean with us. I kept a bucket handy in case an opportunity arose to collect a sample and observe it more closely. I caught a jack-sail-by-the-wind and was amazed at the depth of colour and brilliance of the indigo blue fringe beneath its rigid oval float. The float itself was beautifully patterned with concentric oval lines and ridges fanning out from the base of the sail section. The sail had an aerodynamic twist in it. Apparently some are curved to sail on port tack, others on starboard. This ensures they don't all go in the same direction and pile up, fatally, on the same shore in a long spell of unfavourable winds. I pondered on how many millions of years of trial and error and mutations and near-extinctions and infinitesimal genetic adjustments went into perfecting that one little aid to the survival of that one little species.

I caught a pipe-fish that was lying immobile in the water, impersonating a length of dead marine vegetation. I gave it some minutes to contemplate life in my bucket, where it hung immobile, still impersonating a piece of dead marine vegetation. It didn't look like a fun pet, so I gently returned it to the ocean. I caught and photographed a little swimming crab that waved its paddles at the camera. A well-timed swoop with the bucket scooped up a whole spiral of baby salps, hundreds of them, arranged two by two in the perfect symmetry of a giant coiled spring.

The day wore on. As the sun, if it were in evidence, arced slowly downwards, the look of the sea changed. The swells were always from the west, so that, with the sun now behind them, the approaching faces of the waves moved into deeper and deeper shadow. The featureless flatness of the midday ocean surface was thrown by the changing light into sharper relief. The sea became harder, colder, inimical. It was time to retreat to the cabin, to prepare for the next daily ritual – the 1756 hours weather forecast and the preparation of supper.

My Roberts radio was retrieved from its shelf and unwrapped out of its various leather and plastic casings. A notebook and pencil were produced for taking any notes. Waiting for the approaching forecast, I assembled the main components for the gourmet meal to come. To do this I had first to unscrew the lid of one of the big waterproof containers lashed firmly in several locations around the cabin. Then came the lucky dip. Each container had been filled with the basics for a certain number of meals – how many was written on the container in marker pen. The basics were, typically:

One packet of pre-cooked rice or pasta.
One tin of tuna, or salmon, or smoked oysters.
One tin of peas or beans or carrots or sweetcorn.
One steamed pudding or custard or rice pudding.

If I didn't feel like rice or pasta, I also had a good supply of that marvel of culinary engineering – Smash dried potato. So while waiting for the forecast I delved around and pulled out tins and packets until I had lined up appropriate examples of each component. By then I was already salivating heavily, but had manfully to hold off from starting the cooking until the weather forecast was over.

My one hot meal of the day was designed to combine maximum taste and nourishment with the minimum use of time, effort, fuel and water in its preparation. A typical procedure, designed independently, with no input from, or reference to, any Michelin-starred chef, was:

1. Open tin of peas.
2. Light spirit stove.
3. Drain fluid from peas into small non-stick saucepan.
4. Put saucepan on stove.
5. Add packet of pre-cooked flavoured rice.
6. Add tin of smoked oysters.
7. Add peas.
8. Stir gently for three minutes until piping hot.
9. Turn off stove.
10. Find spoon.
11. Eat.

Quick, simple and delicious. I ate straight from the pan, conserving maximum heat in the food, and keeping wiping up to a minimum. After the main course I was treated to whichever pudding first came to hand in the lucky dip.

The sun wound slowly down to the horizon and I too wound down, preparing myself for a night of on-off sleep. During the darkening evening I stretched out and dozed a little, my little kitchen timer tucked close to my ear. I had a hurricane lamp hanging in the cabin, but now only used it in really cold weather, to generate some warmth. My port and starboard navigation lights, set into the coach-roof sides, diffused the cabin with a faint ambient light. Along with the bright stern light, which reflected off the shiny alloy of the steering gear, they gave good illumination, soft and inoffensive to night vision, for working on deck in the dark. If I needed a stronger light for chart-work or writing up the ship's log, or, as happened several times, repairing corroded switches in the wiring loom, I used an LED headlamp.

With night almost upon us, I switched on the navigation lights. What comfort they gave, with their incredible brightness in the engulfing gloom, their powering energy drawn silently from the daytime sun. My solar panel was tiny, but drew enough sustenance from the ether to power my lights night after night, with never a moment's pause.

Night was a round of sleep, wake and check, then sleep, wake and check. The wind was as fitful during the night as the day, so I was on deck regularly, adjusting the wind vane and our sail trim. Once or twice fishing boats were working nearby, mooching around in unpredictable meanderings. I could then not risk sleeping and often sat uncomfortably in the hatch way, where the chances of dropping off to sleep in the cold air were pretty much zero, watching until their lights were the merest pinpricks, winking faintly on and off as they fell below the horizon. After a swig of water, and perhaps an energy bar if I was feeling peckish, it was back to my bunk and another round of sleep, wake and check.

Sometimes the rhythm enabled me to catch the early morning weather forecast, around five thirty, sometimes it didn't. I wasn't that bothered whether I heard it or not. We would get the weather we were going to get, whatever the forecast may say. The forecasts were anyway quite inaccurate, particularly in FitzRoy. I developed a healthy scepticism:

A weather forecaster one day
Announced in an off-handish way:
'We may well get rain, but then again
Could be dry – you never can say...'

The night dissolved imperceptibly, allowing the steely grey Atlantic dawn to force its way through the port-lights. Drained of all colour, the sea and sky, first thing, encircled us with a cold and clammy death pall. The start of the day, under a lowering charcoal sky, was rarely welcoming. I stayed below, warm under my sleeping bag, the hatch shut, until an intimation of sunlight and the day proper shamed me to get up and get moving. It was time to think of breakfast, time to wash and tidy, time for another new day.

16

Bit by patient bit, always close-hauled into the inconsistent northerly air stream, often so comprehensively becalmed that I lowered the mainsail and lashed it to the deck to stop the relentless slatting, we worked our way back towards soundings and the western approaches. By 25th June, our twenty-third day at sea, we were closing the two-hundred-metre depth contour. Our noon position put us a mere twenty-five miles off the edge of the Little Sole Bank, round about two hundred miles south-west of the Lizard. We still had our patchy wind from the north-west, but for once I was quite happy about that. Many a returning yachtsman, and, more recently, oarsman, has come a cropper hereabouts. The sea floor shoals rapidly from four thousand metres to a mere two hundred, setting up all manner of currents and turbulences. Combine that with a nasty north Atlantic blow and you have a recipe for a very dangerous sea. My aim in following the weather forecasts had principally been to have some advance warning of any deep incoming depressions. If necessary I would delay the final run in. Now there was no need. There was no heavy weather in prospect; we had about one hundred nautical miles sea room between us and the dangerous Brittany coast; the sea was in a benign frame of mind.

Confirmation that we were indeed on soundings came at

ten thirty that evening, as we breached the line of a fleet of Spanish drift-netters spread horizon to horizon. *Where are the lads from Grimsby?* I thought ruefully as, like Nelson at Trafalgar, we cut midway through the Spanish position. A cold and patchy northerly wind continued on, while the forecasters kept promising a Force 4 from the south. A wind from the south! A following wind! A fair breeze to waft us up-Channel! Ah, how I dreamed of that balmy zephyr! For several days it was dangled in front of our twitching noses – the juicy unattainable carrot. We never got a bite at it.

As we haltingly closed the land, still enduring regular patches of total calm, we saw more and more ships and fishing boats. At nine fifteen on the evening of the 27th June a French fishing boat, *Le Derby* – make of that what you will – crossed our bows so close that it had to accelerate noisily to avoid a collision. He won the race by a short head. Early next morning a great white cruise ship, lit up like an octogenarian's birthday cake, passed astern, heading west. I thought of its thousands of passengers, at five thirty on a cold Atlantic dawn still snoring under their hot duvets, exchanging morning-after breath with their blue-rinsed partners, and dreaming of the great life on the ocean wave. Later that morning a fine looking container ship, the *Haruna Express* of St John's, painted such a startling shade of powder blue as to appear almost coquettish, passed us half a mile on the starboard beam, also heading west. For no apparent reason a Lear jet, or something like it, appeared from the east, made a couple of low circuits around the ship, then flew off whence it had come.

By noon that day we were within thirty miles of the Lizard. The North Atlantic Ocean Passage Chart was put away for good, as we transferred to the Admiralty Western Approaches sheet. Under the hot, hazy afternoon sun I searched the northern horizon. By four thirty it was certain that the low finger of darker grey, bearing slightly east of north, was land. Within an hour it had resolved clearly into the Land's End peninsula, with Land's End itself now quite visible directly to the north. It was our first sight of land for twenty-five days or so, and as if to underline our return to civilisation, or at any rate to human proximity, I got a friendly wave from the skipper of a fishing boat, registration P29, who passed close by shooting his nets.

The landfall provoked little excitement. Why should it? With satellite-aided navigation it was a humdrum, banal affair, devoid of the tension, satisfaction and sometimes almost wonder, of making a good landfall, after weeks at sea, with celestial workings only.

It was nonetheless a beautiful evening. The soft Cornish hills stretched out to the north and, as we moved slowly east in the gentle breeze, the white dish aerials of Goonhilly Downs glowed in the early-evening sun. The focus of all our efforts for the last two weeks, the Lizard, rose slowly above the horizon, still lying immobile and statuesque, still crouched long and low, the sleeping, inscrutable sentinel. It was a strange sensation, eating my evening meal, to glance through the port-light and see land. But it meant that our world was once again shrinking. We were being squeezed into a narrow, crowded corridor. The open horizon was gone. Possibility was now inflexibly finite. I had to be on my toes. Land and big ships once more threatened.

17

My first log entry for the 29th June, made at one thirty in the morning, continued the theme that had become so constant and all-pervading that it was becoming difficult to imagine life otherwise:

0130 Becalmed. Off the Lizard...Beautiful starry night though.

Becalmed! How many times had I written that word over the preceding weeks! I could not shake it off. By dawn, on a sea as flat and unruffled as a Claridges' table cloth, we had been pushed back west and south by the ebb tide. However I was determined that we would weather the Lizard that day. To the west of the Lizard our options were limited. Once to the east there were plenty of safe havens, should the weather break. That was an unlikely prospect, with the forecasts now settled into a procession of Variable 3's – weatherman code for *'We're sorry, we haven't a clue'* – but as our sea room evaporated, we had to be ready for every eventuality. When the light breeze came it had, with an insouciant spitefulness that now seemed inevitable, hauled round into the east. The northerlies, that had tortured us for weeks but would now serve well as we turned up-Channel, had thrown us a last *'Ta-ra, whack'* and pushed off elsewhere. *Thanks a lot.*

We were back to headlands and tide-gates, and I was back to occasional bouts of hand-steering, if necessary, to help force us through the difficult nodes. With a light head wind and an awkward northerly set to the flood tide, it took all morning and all afternoon to work our way past the Lizard. It was only a brief and fortuitous wind shift to the south that freed us up enough to creep past, well within the bubbling but unthreatening tide race. As we left Black Head astern I breathed easier. With the land falling away to the north, towards Falmouth, we had earned a little sea room, enough that I could relax, put *Mingming* back onto self-steering, tidy up ship, and sleep. The wind settled back to a light east-south-easterly, and we trundled along steadily through another warm and starlit night.

The early morning forecast proposed winds from the north-east. I could sense yet another period of adversity creeping up on us. North-easterlies generated by a big, slow-moving high-pressure system, which is what seemed to be on the cards, could blow for days and days, often quite strongly. There was no way I could breach the Portland Bill tide-gate in a strong north-easterly. Everything might be reversed quite symmetrically from my passage the other way. Moreover, the wide expanses of Lyme Bay were not particularly hospitable for a small engine-less yacht, with few viable bolt-holes in heavy weather. Ah well. There was no point yet in getting too exercised about it, but I was already considering possible strategies just in case we did have a lengthy north-easterly blow.

However, for the time being, we had at last what really could be termed a balmy zephyr, edging back and forth between south and south-east. As long as you were not in too much of a hurry, it was an idyllic day. A warm and almost-adequate breeze ruffled the gently pulsing surface of a sea as uncompromisingly blue as the unblemished sky. A warm haze was enough to soften the horizon, but not enough to veil the bold West Country headlands to the north, or the townships tucked modestly amongst them – Megavissey, St Austell and the like.

Nor was the haze enough to hide the rash of yachts that appeared after breakfast time, scooting like mad hatters to inviolate appointments, mainsails hard amidships, engines a-roar. They somehow sadden me, these sailors who reach unswervingly for the starter button if conditions don't give them instant hull speed, whose passages are a constant ugly rush to overpower, literally, whatever wind or water may oppose them, who are ruled by timetables inimical to the ebb and flow of nature and for whom to be still, calm and immobile on a gentle sea amounts to an affront to their tortured hyperactivity.

Then suddenly – an apparition! To the north-west, ghostlike, the neatly squared and tightly furled spars of a three-masted ship, almost hull down, moved through the haze, then dropped from view. A fat little guillemot flew urgently by. Eddystone Light materialised on the starboard bow. A yacht appeared ahead coming straight for us. We passed just fifty yards apart, with a lazy wave. A fishing boat crossed our bows, leaving a dismaying trail of detritus – plastic drinks bottles, rubbish bags, tins, food packaging – a good week's worth of assorted refuse, in its wake. I spat metaphorically over the side and looked the other way, where a big double-ended cruising yacht by the name of *John Benn* was overtaking us, Plymouth-bound, mainsail hard amidships and engine a-roar. Was there no end to this breathless activity, this great hustle and bustle of the inshore traffic zone?

By five that afternoon we had passed the Eddystone Light and crossed, I thought then for the last time, our outward track from Plymouth, laid down exactly twenty-seven days previously. As Plymouth Sound had opened up, slowly revealing the distant town itself, bathed in the pulsating heat of the afternoon sun, my good humour had faltered. Where were they now – the nine other skippers who had sailed out of here just a few weeks before? Our camaraderie, almost palpable, had been scattered, literally, to the four winds. Would we ever re-group? Or was it just one chance collision of like-minded adventurers? Were there now nine yachts converging on Newport, with just *Mingming* creeping painfully home?

I didn't know. I had no way of knowing, and until I had completed the business in hand and sailed *Mingming* safely back to her mooring, I really did not want to know. That was for later. Nevertheless the memories and feelings provoked by the sight of our point of departure underlined how fleeting and irrevocable are our human inter-weavings, and set off a brief bout of emptiness and regret at it all.

Plymouth. Singular town that it is, an addictive mix of the pretty, the rough and the chaotic, it had pained me to see it again, so unexpectedly soon. I didn't want to go there and be reminded of so much that had been lost so quickly. Nature, whose insensate will is rarely to be argued with, had other ideas. After another warm night lying in our habitual calm somewhere between the Eddystone Light and Start Point, a breeze came up from east-north-east. *Ugh.* Having been set as far to the south as I was prepared to go during the night, I tacked north. With the ebb pushing us, this was in effect north-west. By eight in the morning, as the wind once more failed, we were lying just five miles south of Plymouth breakwater. The arms of the Sound were now opened wide to welcome us in. *No! No!* I tacked south again, retracing our morning board. The forecast was still for north-easterlies. It would be hard to weather Start Point. Maybe I could find a spot somewhere along the coast between Plymouth and Prawle Point to lie to anchor and await a fairer wind.

Noon came, and with it the strangest irony. We had been at sea for exactly four weeks. We had sailed over two thousand miles, mostly tortuous miles in perversely fickle headwinds and calms. I measured carefully on the chart. We were just eight miles from our starting point.

For the moment the wind was from east-south-east. I stood in to Bigbury Bay, to get a feel for the conditions close inshore. With the breeze blowing more or less parallel to the coast it was clear that none of the exposed anchoring spots along that stretch of coast would be tenable. On the other hand it would take a prodigious effort to weather Start Point with this headwind. Even if I could do it, which was doubtful, it would simply put us right into the path of the forecast north-easterlies, with, potentially, a lee shore under us.

18

Plymouth. I really did not want to go in there, but in the end I had no real choice. At two thirty on that Saturday afternoon I dropped anchor on the outside of the jostling crowd of weekend yachts in Jennycliff Bay. This little bay, quite pretty with its wooded slopes, sits on the east side of Plymouth Harbour, just inside the eastern entrance. Although exposed to the south-west, it was ideal for sheltering from a north-easterly blow.

We lay there until early on Monday morning. All around was the great weekend bustle of Plymouth Harbour – life as usual. I felt quite disconnected from it, but watched it all with the greatest fascination. I was still, after all, voyaging, with the mindset of the voyager. What was this strange civilisation I had chanced upon? All day, fast and noisy little boats roared round and round us, dangerously close, dragging, by means of long ropes, straining men and women dressed in tight-fitting rubber clothes. Was it some weird initiation rite? It was evidently a joyful experience for them, with much laughter, shouting and banter between the high priests driving the boats, and the initiates risking life and limb behind them. They seemed to be of a different sect from the natives sedately at anchor in their local sailing craft. These boats were uniformly white, sleek and shiny, of copious dimensions and well loaded with all manner of bizarre contrivances and wondrous accoutrements whose utility was hard to fathom. The natives aboard these craft seemed strangely subdued compared to their exuberant compatriots of the boat-dragging-man sect. Mostly they lounged quietly on plush cushions in the outside living rooms at the back end of their boats. Under cleverly contrived covers to shade them from the hot rays of the midday sun, they sat around finely-fashioned teak tables, drinking well-fermented brews and reading their sacred texts. Sometimes, and I suspect here some religious significance, they divested themselves of near-ly all their clothes and lay immodestly on a flat space of deck, offering themselves, perhaps, to some Zoroastrian deity. I desisted from any intercourse with these strange natives, pre-ferring to keep my counsel and observe them and their exot-ic practices from a polite distance.

The reluctant decision to lie to anchor and await a fair wind was soon vindicated. By six on that Saturday evening it was gusting strongly from the north-east, with great willi-waws swooping down off the steep slopes to windward. Throughout the night we were assaulted physically and aurally by bouts of thunder, lightning and torrential rain. The day sailors having vacated most of the anchorage, I could have moved in closer to a more sheltered spot, but I stayed where I was. I was unlikely to be boxed in and had plenty of room to sail off my anchor. In any event, if the anchorage became untenable, it was only a favourable wind that would make it so, so I would be leaving anyway.

Plymouth. Sunday 2nd July.

1100 I spend an idle half hour with the binoculars observing life in Plymouth Harbour; quite a few yachts, mostly over-canvassed in the gusty wind; a weird-looking navy ship L308, shepherded on to a mooring buoy by a police launch and two tugs; background left, travesties of sixties architecture – three high-rise blocks of social housing; background centre, work in progress on a number of travesties of twenty-first century architecture – smart apartment blocks with sea views and views on other smart apartment blocks with sea views; centre stage leftish, the tall box-like structure, a cross between a grain silo, a mausoleum and the Liverpool Anglican cathedral, that dominates and ruins the flow and scale of that part of the waterfront. Then a bright spot: a Cornish lugger, registration PZ111, with tan sails and an extraordinary purple hull, sails past easily under jib and mizzen. The classic effect is moderated somewhat by the self-steering gear on the transom and the rubber dinghy towed astern. She heads off to the western entrance. Where bound? Looe perhaps, to commune with other luggers...

1500 A tranquil day continues. I have cleaned, tidied, rearranged this and that, broken out the more inaccessible food containers and revived the selection of gourmet treats available, refilled the stove, refilled my water bottles, added four stanzas to 'The Odyssey of Mr & Mrs Newley-Richards', studied boat life in Plymouth, checked out alternative anchorages if need be, kept my ship's log going, taken the plaster off the burn (Strippit) on my head, counted the boats at anchor (thirty-one), controlled all annoyance and incipient cursing at passing water-skiers, avoided the temptation to take a little siesta. In short, a triumph of a day...

1530 A little band of sea kayakers passes by, doing it

the hard way. They make me feel quite ashamed of my indiscriminate use of wind power to get around.

1720 An adult and an immature guillemot drift by quite close on the dying ebb, attending attentively to their preening and oiling. The anchorage grows emptier as one by one the yachts and powerboats are forced home by the imperatives of an imminent Monday morning. Will I be the sole survivor?

2000 Patience is rewarded with perfect tranquillity. The dying sun glints over a smooth and strangely deserted harbour. A lone yacht straggles home. Not a powerboat in sight or sound. Bliss...

2035 Spoke a fraction too soon. This I do not believe! The biggest, plushest, sleekest, most expensive-look-ing 'yacht' i.e. private ship, the Samar of George Town, *has just purred in and dropped anchor a hun-dred yards away. It has its own private helicopter on board, for heaven's sake. At least four decks above the waterline. Fruiting orange trees and palms on the after decks. A good two hundred and fifty feet and worth millions. The peaceful mood is now destroyed, as I wonder if they will send over a boat to invite me to dinner, and if so, which tuxedo I'll wear...Or maybe I could invite them over for drinks and canapes. We could compare interiors. Enough...*

2200 I set the riding light and turn in.

19

I cleared out of Plymouth very early the next morning. When I woke at five thirty the light wind had a lot of north in it – a good wind for Prawle Point. There was an hour or so of ebb left to help me out, then the east-going flood. It was too seductive to refuse. Irrespective of the weather I just had to get sailing again. In addition, I really did not want to spend another minute in the shadow of the opulent behemoth anchored alongside, bathed in the self-satisfied glow of its own smug vulgarity.

With a fair wind and the tide under us we raced southeast along the coast towards Salcombe and Start Point. Despite the wind swinging back to east-north-east, and freshening as we cleared the headlands, we had, by early afternoon, come close to weathering Start Point and poking our nose into Lyme Bay. But this voyage had its fixed rhythm, and would not be deterred from it. The wind fell away to nothing. We lay rolling under a hot and murky sky, becalmed for the umpteenth time, with the tide about to turn and carry us back west. Oh well. I hardly cared. By now I was so inured to adversity, so hardened to the inevitability of the constant setback, that I met it all with a philosophical shrug.

I was rewarded for my sangfroid. Within a short time a little breeze popped up from the south-east, a good leading wind for our next target well to the south of Portland Bill. It became a fine beam wind, a perfect sailing breeze, for one hour, before resuming the gyrations we knew so well. It didn't matter. We had worked our way sufficiently to the east, over the ebb tide, so that Start Point was comprehensively behind us. To the north-west, through the evening murk, I could make out Berry Head and the approaches to Dartmouth. We stood on as best we could across Lyme Bay, playing the fickle winds. A lone guillemot accompanied us for a while, diving for food almost alongside. I timed a dive – one minute fifty-two seconds. Impressive, given his, or her, tiny lungs and the effort required to chase prey under water.

During the night the inimitable breathy explosions of dolphins expelling air through their blowholes brought me to the hatch, as did, from time to time, the purr and hum and throb of ships' engines, resonating almost imperceptibly through the hull and putting me on alert. The early morning forecaster talked of westerly winds for Plymouth and Portland. The man was obviously mad. Towards seven, as we ghosted eastwards in the faintest of zephyrs on a pristine sea, a little coaster, the *Hoodcrest* of London, heading north-east, crossed close across our bows. I peered at the officer of the watch, snug in his wheelhouse, with my binoculars. He fetched his binoculars and peered back. For a minute or two we held each other's lens-enhanced gaze, seeing who would blink first.

Then suddenly – an apparition! To the north-west, the neatly squared and tightly furled spars of a three-masted ship, almost hull down, was moving parallel to us through the haze. A wasp flew in and tried to open one of my Fox's glacier mints. A puff came up from south-south-west, then abandoned us. It grew hotter and hotter.

1150 Through the murk to the north west I spot the

long white hull and three masts of a white-hulled three-masted ship – under full sail! Yessir, royals, skysails, moonrakers, staysails, studding sails alow and aloft. It is now glassy smooth and searingly hot:

> *A weary time! A weary time!*
> *There was nor breath nor motion.*
> *Thank God the dear old captain's chest*
> *Was full of suntan lotion.*

The noon weather forecaster too was evidently infected with the outbreak of certifiable madness at the Met Office. He too talked blithely of south-west winds, Force 3 to 4. It was sad, sad…

> *Twenty-three common gulls hold an informal floating colloquy a few yards off my stern. Beyond them, ghostly on the horizon, the three-masted ship, yards braced to windward, staysails and jibs close-hauled, romps nostalgically to windward on the non-existent breeze.*

All afternoon we chased the wind round, always after the best heading, an almost pointless exercise, given the minimal benefit at the ghosting speeds we were achieving. Things looked brighter later on as a Force 2 south-south-easterly came in, allowing us to sail well and freely on our proper heading, and a fishing boat, registration OB454, jauntily painted in blue and white, passed by on the starboard beam, heading west. Within two hours the good breeze had dropped away to nothing. I was not surprised:

> *Think! In this battered caravanserai*
> *Whose doorways are alternate night and day,*

How many bossy little breezes blew
Then, leaving us to languish, went their way.

Despite the interminable jilling about, we were by then halfway across Lyme Bay. The decision to leave Jennycliff Bay and get on with it seemed to have paid off. However we were now approaching the tricky problem of the Portland Bill tide-gate. As the Channel narrowed and the long spit of Portland funnelled the currents, the tides progressively increased. We had a smooth sea. All we needed was a fair wind to keep us moving east over the ebb tides. At least we were not far from neaps, so we would avoid the strong spring tide currents that had tormented us on our journey the other way.

The madmen at the Met Office, confirmed in their pitiable lunacy, still had a fixation about the imminence of a south-west wind. We had been at sea for thirty-two days and had scarcely encountered such a thing. The south-west wind had gone. It was no more. The south-west wind was dead. We would never again experience the blustery dampness of a well-formed and spritely south-west wind. Never again, ever.

20

A gyrating westerly did come, after all, but it came reluctantly, and it came well-loaded with thunder and lightning, calm patches and squalls and great banks of fog. It was a messy and uncomfortable lump of weather, but it kept us pushing east all night, and by five in the morning we were due south of Portland Bill, about eight miles off.

I had broken out the foghorn and kept up the regulation token blasts, elephantine trumpetings that got soaked up in the great porous fog and were rewarded with neither reply nor echo. It was doubly a vain exercise, this brazen announcement of our presence to the wholly uncaring world around us, that had no chance, anyway, of reaching the ears it needed to – the ears of sleepy officers of the watch cocooned in their warm bridge decks and lulled to insouciant deafness by the purrings of the great diesels beneath. But I kept it up, because you must.

At nine that morning, out of the gloom behind, came a Thames bawley, L1247, topsail set, wrestling with the same problems of rain squalls and fickle gusts. It slowly overtook us, a hundred yards on the port beam, and disappeared into the murk ahead. It was strangely comforting to trek along for a short while with this outrider from the east coast mud. We were making progress homewards, after all.

By noon we were south of St Alban's Head, still in a fog

that could not decide whether to be a good old pea-souper, or something a little lighter, more nouvelle cuisine. Not long before, a massive angular container ship had passed us fairly close going west, not bothering with its foghorn, and evidently at full steam ahead in the minimal visibility. *May the captain's progeny and all their issue forever be walking into lampposts!*

With this first fair wind for weeks we kept on just north of east, aiming to pass comfortably to the south of St Catherine's Point. It was a shame that for this first passage to the outside of the Isle of Wight there was little chance of seeing much of it.

My noon game with the dividers confirmed that Caracas was now a good distance to the south-west. On the other hand we were now midway between Land's End and the South Foreland. It was a long job, but we were getting there. My postprandial nap was interrupted by a low-flying helicopter that scared the living bejaysus out of me. *May the pilot's progeny and all their issue forever be falling out of bed!*

Later that afternoon we experienced the most unexpected and miraculous phenomenon. I was not hallucinating. It was a fact. We were sailing with a proper, unequivocal, steady Force 4 south-westerly, beautifully positioned on our starboard quarter and propelling us at our sprightliest lick of the whole voyage. Some more playing with the dividers showed that at this rate the South Foreland was only a day away. We could even, conceivably, reach Burnham-on-Crouch within two days. Ah, Burnham:

> *There was an old sailor from Burnham,*
> *Whose wife's chest was as flat as her sternum.*
> *She'd enhance her small-and-tenders with a couple*
>   *of fenders,*
> *'Til they docked, when she had to return 'em.*

By seven thirty we were south of St Catherine's Point. The fog relented enough to give us a glimpse of the lighthouse buildings and a vague impression of the landmass looming behind. Despite a freshening breeze from astern the ebb tide was working its poison, pinning us to the south-east corner of the island.

For that night we just needed one more big effort, on the imminent flood, to cross the eastern approaches of the Solent, crowded as they are with all manner of shipping, and get ourselves beyond the dangers of the Outer Owers banks. The fog was now lifting for a while, unveiling the twinkling lights of the east Isle of Wight towns, and the steaming lights of the ships plying the waters wherever I looked, then suddenly dropping on us again, a black, suffocating sack, woven tight and unyielding around us.

I dozed on and off, played the foghorn in the fog, watched the shipping when it was watchable. By the time an unconvincing simulacrum of a summer dawn was trying to pierce the choking gloom around us, we were nine miles due south of Selsey Bill, borne by the flood tide and a following wind away from the shipping, almost past the Outer Owers, still holding our course of eighty magnetic that would lead us on to Beachy Head and the Royal Sovereign Light and all points east. On we went in the featureless all-encompassing grey, which lightened only reluctantly as the morning wore on, and ticked off one by one those resonant south coast towns – Bognor, Worthing, Littlehampton, Shoreham, all unseen but each, I felt, nodding slightly in acknowledgement as we rewound our dogged way back to the mud flats and swatch-ways.

The featureless morning continues. The only points of interest since dawn have been the passing of a catamaran going north-west on a beam reach, main-

sail reefed, and an abundance of cuttlefish bones in the water. I whiled away a bit of time thinking up a rhyme about cuttlefish, but, as Editor of the Ship's Log, sent a brief rejection slip to myself. It is brightening up very slightly, and visibility is gradually improving, but no land yet in sight.

On we went, and in the early afternoon the unmistakable chalky folds of the Seven Sisters cliffs, little more than an ethereal blur through the persistent mist, confirmed, at last, that our course was true. Beachy Head materialised on our port beam, but my attention was elsewhere. Ahead was the distinctive dark shape of a gaff-rigged mainsail. It was a good distance away, but as I studied it a strange and unlikely proposition asserted itself – *we were gaining on it*. I was wary at first. Was this simply an illusion brought on by close proximity to a suicidal headland? Had thirty-four days at sea scrambled my brains? Was it no more than a triumph of unbridled optimism over sad reality? *Mingming*, in general, does not do overtaking. That is not her role in life. My silent incantation, as the sleek and shiny whizzkids show us their dismissive stern-wave, is always – *You may go faster, matey, but I'll go a damn sight further...*

But after a half-hour or so of intense assessment of the now-not-quite-so-tiny tan sail ahead there was no doubt about it. We were winding her in, painfully slowly admittedly, but winding her in we were. It is truly disgraceful how the thought of actually passing the man ahead can galvanise you (all right, me) into a lather of sail trimming and gleeful expectancy. We were gaining, and I was damn well going to make sure that we kept on gaining.

It took us two hours to get up to the puzzling sailing craft ahead – puzzling because it became clear that she was in fact quite sizeable, not the minnow I had at first assumed, and from a distance had an odd look to her that had me thinking for a while that she may be a Dutch barge. As we drew level with her, a hundred yards on her starboard beam, with both of us just about to round the Royal Sovereign Light on its great concrete tower, the mystery was revealed. She was about forty-five feet of Polperro hooker, *Attica* POL2018, with a distinctive black hull and deep bulwarks. She was badly in need of her topsail to give her some extra push, but the guys on board were evidently not rushed.

Slowly we overhauled her. I studied the fine old working boat with my binoculars; *Attica's* crew studied the odd little junk-rigged upstart passing them with their binoculars. I thought about her pretty name – *Attica, Attica...* Before too long a recordable, though less than perfect, idea came to mind:

There was a young hooker called Attica
Who read Newton's 'Principia Mathematica'
To master the notions of physical motions
And make her men even ecstaticker.

On we went, gradually losing the lovely and carnally accomplished *Attica* in the mists astern. Our target was now Dungeness. With what was now almost a westerly wind from dead astern, and the flood tide under us, we should be there before midnight. I had by now been sailing alone along the south coast for nearly ninety hours and felt I needed to refresh myself before the difficult final leg around the South Foreland and across the Thames Estuary. Although I was loath to waste a fair wind, I knew that a couple of hours of uninterrupted sleep would pay off later on.

As we closed the Dungeness headland in, once again, thick fog and a freshening breeze that forced a reefing of the mainsail, I decided to pull round into the lee of the spit, into

Dungeness East Roads. Fortuitously the fog lifted just as we altered course to pass to leeward of the lighthouse, making location of the ideal spot to anchor that much easier. The shallow water here, with its hard sandy bottom, provides a surprisingly placid anchorage in westerly weather. By eleven that night, in perfect tranquillity under a luminous and sharp-edged moon, I was rocked gently into the depths of satisfied sleep. Our voyage, I thought, as a few hours of blissful oblivion descended, was nearly over. We may even be home tomorrow. The difficulties were all behind us.

How wrong I was. How very wrong and stupid to assume that nature, that rigorous and fickle master, would not provide a final kick in the teeth to test our mettle. I slept well, happily ignorant that the worst and most difficult night of our whole voyage still lay ahead.

21

By five thirty the next morning I had got our anchor and we were under way under full mainsail in a light south-westerly. High water would be about four hours later. With luck and a fair wind we may be able to take the last of the flood up-Channel, then pick up the ebb tide north past Deal and Ramsgate. That was the plan, but as the light wind faltered my confidence in achieving it eroded. The timing was critical. If we did not cross the node between the east/west Channel tides and the north/south North Sea tides in time, the ebb flow would be against us.

For a while I hand-steered to help us along. Still the weather alternated between spells of milky sunshine and thicker mist. The sun, when it shone, albeit weakly, turned the sea a deep green, a striking contrast to the recent greys and indigos of the pelagic waters. We ran close along a line of lobster pots and got a friendly wave from the two crewmen of the little lobster boat, FE49, which was working them. For once the coast was clear, with the cliffs of Folkestone standing stolidly a mile or two on our port beam. I could feel a strong tide pushing us, but was as yet unsure whether it was the last of the flood, or the start of the ebb north.

By nine thirty, as Folkestone approached rapidly to port, there was no doubt. We were on the conveyor belt! We had been picked up by the great mass of water draining north, pushed and pulled by the gargantuan and unfathomable forces of planetary attraction. We had achieved the optimum strategy for passing from the Channel to the North Sea, stealing a free ride on the tides for at least ten hours at a single stretch. We were racing. Within scarcely more than an hour Dover was passed and the South Foreland, that great white chalky shoulder that marks the passage out of the Dover Strait, was abeam. Farewell Atlantic! Goodbye Channel! Hello North Sea!

We came round the corner into a smooth sea, and as we came round the wind too hauled into the south and freshened. We creamed along, the tide strengthening under us, ecstatic at finally having every element in our favour. I could not resist checking our ground speed on the hand-held GPS. Seven knots! The mist had evaporated and we sped up past the Georgian elegance of Deal's waterfront in crisp sunshine, with still four hours of the ebb tide left to carry us. What a homecoming! What a run!

By three in the afternoon we were off the North Foreland, with the expanses of the Thames stretching away to the west, but the weather had collapsed. After an hour or two of squalls and byzantine rainstorms we were once again becalmed in a lumpy east coast slop. The last of the ebb carried us gently seawards. A hesitant south-east zephyr helped us north for a short while, then died.

On our first night out from Burnham we had lain right here in thick fog. I sat in the hatchway and, resigned once more to the inescapable stop-go-stop rhythm of the voyage, watched what little there was to watch. To the north-east a big red cargo ship paraded back and forth in some inexplicable manoeuvrings. One or two yachts motored past at a distance, mainsails hard amidships, engines a-roar. A sleek and anorexic yellow trimaran, no doubt contesting the Round Britain and Ireland Race, fought its way painfully south, to seawards of us. The slop smoothed out. I ate my pan of basmati rice with tuna and sweetcorn. I wondered whether we would spend the night here, wafted back and forth on the tide.

At seven thirty an excellent breeze sprang up from the south-west and had us scooting north towards Fisherman's Gat in smooth water. This wide, buoyed southern swatchway would lead us in to the intricacies of the Thames sandbanks. With the wind holding I found and passed through the Gat, exiting into the Black Deep channel just as darkness fell. In *Mingming*, with her shallow draft, I usually cross the next sandbank, the Sunk, at the Sunk Beacon itself, rather than at the generally favoured South-West Sunk Beacon. Once out of Fisherman's Gat, I therefore turned due north to take us across Black Deep towards the Sunk. Once we reached 51 40N, an hour or so later, I altered course due west to head past the beacon, over the shallows and into the next channel, Barrow Deep.

It was now a black, moonless night. We crossed the Sunk Sand, still with a leading wind. Through the gloom I could just make out the darker shape of the unlit Sunk Beacon tower as it slid past to starboard. It was now almost exactly high tide. As we moved out into Barrow Deep I felt ecstatic. The Sunk Sand is for me the symbolic barrier between the south and north Thames estuary. Once over it, we were truly into home waters. From here we could sail home with no more sandbanks to cross. We could simply sail due west into the East Swin, and on to the mouth of the Whitaker Channel. This leads straight into the approaches to the River Crouch, and home.

We had come so far together, *Mingming* and I, battling down-Channel to Plymouth, then out nearly a thousand miles into the north Atlantic, then back, retracing our track into the incessant headwinds, always battling doggedly on, taking whatever came as even-mindedly as we could, persevering day after day to make a few miles of progress and shape this little voyage into a worthwhile adventure. We were now just twenty miles or so from home with, it seemed, every obstacle behind us. A warm joy suffused every cell in my body. Just twenty more miles to go.

We were scarcely across Barrow Deep and moving into the waters of the East Swin when nature dealt out its final backhander, a well-aimed and stinging swipe across the cheek that brought metaphorical tears to my eyes. Take that. And that. Within a few seconds the wind pulled round straight to the west and jumped up several notches in strength. Our leading wind had gone. Our smooth sea built rapidly to an awkward chop. The tide turned.

Safely across the Sunk. Could just make out the beacon in the gloom (it is not lit). However, things are now getting difficult. The wind has hauled into the west, and strengthened considerably. To get across to the approaches to the River Crouch, or indeed the Blackwater, I have to go due west. I now have wind and tide against me, and a nasty Thames sea building. There is no way I can make progress forward. I am effectively stuck in the East Swin for the night. Gunfleet Sand to the north, Sunk Sand to the south, the Foulness, Buxey and East Barrow Sands to the south-west. A real Maurice Griffiths' moment. All I can do is wait for the next flood tide at 0500 tomorrow morning. However I cannot, obviously, anchor, so what to do? Either tack endlessly back and forth, trying to hold my position until morning, or simply heave-to. The problem is I have already been at the tiller for most of the last eighteen hours from Dungeness. I would then have to do another six hours all night, then continue once the tide has turned. The problem with heaving-to is we are then pushed back by wind and tide at one and a half to two knots, all distance that will have to be made up again in the morning, wasting much if not most of the fair tide.

22

I in no way regretted having pressed on across the estuary as night fell – I had to keep moving – but I was now in an awkward bind. The worst aspect was that I could not allow myself even a minute's sleep. I simply could not risk not being woken by my alarms. At our rate of drift, and with sandbanks all around us, even a slight wind shift could push us onto hard sand within an hour or two. Whether I was on deck or below, there was one priority. Keep awake!

It was a long, hard, cold and horrible night. I spent as much time as I could on deck, beating back and forth into the short, steep seas. With a concentrated effort I could make some progress to windward, gauging our position off the incessant taunting winks of the channel buoys and cardinal markers ranged around us. But from time to time I needed some respite from the cold, and from the sleep-inducing boredom of our endless rhythmic punching into the chop. Each time I came below I dropped the mainsail and lay-to. I could not risk sailing under self-steering. If I dropped off we would be aground in no time.

Below I studiously occupied myself with any task that would not induce sleep. Keep awake! I checked and rechecked our position. I slapped my cheeks. I yelled at myself. Keep awake! Each period below saw us lose all our gains to windward and more. When I could face it once again

I hauled up the mainsail for another hour on deck beating back and forth, back and forth, fighting an overall losing battle to hold our position, ready for the flood tide. It was by now blowing a good Force 6.

As the first hints of the false dawn lightened the sky almost imperceptibly, just after four in the morning, I once more resumed the task on deck. There was now just an hour of the ebb to run. Perhaps we could now start to make some real progress. For a short while we plugged to windward once more, losing our guiding lights one by one as day came. Ahead was now a wide and angry expanse of windswept grey sea and sky, uninviting, monochromatic, grim. I had not slept for twenty-four hours. Although the pilotage was not difficult, I was no longer wholly confident that in my tired state I would not make a mistake. From where we now were, well out in the East Swin, it would take, realistically, two flood tides to get us home, with another six hour holding operation in between – anything up to eighteen hours in all. Suddenly I realised I did not have the stomach or the physical capacity for another long day at the helm, in these conditions. I had fought gamely all night to hold our position, but it was as much as I could do. It was time to throw in the towel.

Reluctantly, but knowing it was the only sensible choice open to me, I played our get-out card. It had always been there, ready to be employed if need be. The engine-less sailor must always, always have an escape plan, a fallback position. I would never have crossed the Sunk Sand without an alternative route out of the encircling sandbanks. I put the helm up to run north-east up the East Swin, along the eastern side of the Gunfleet Sand. Eventually the shoal waters on our port beam would give out, and we could turn north-west to run past Harwich and into the Orwell River. It broke my heart to turn our head away from home, now so tantalisingly close, and run north to the Suffolk rivers. But with a quartering wind the sailing was fast and easy. In four or five hours' time I could anchor, sleep, and await a fair wind back down the coast and home.

By ten we were anchored at Stone Heaps, just a few hundred yards inside the mouth of the Orwell River proper, on the west side. It is a strange, schizophrenic spot that we have used many times over the years. Look one way and you have a rural Suffolk idyll of soft rolling countryside. Look the other, just a few yards across the river to the north-east, and you are overpowered by the massive angular structures of the Felixstowe container wharf and the long line of slab-sided ships forever muscling in and out of their tight berths, pushed and pulled by the powerful little tugs that serve them. The wharf seems to be under continuous construction, pushing further and further up the east bank of the river.

But that morning, once I was happy that my anchor was well set, and was about to turn in for some desperately needed sleep, a third and unexpected visual marvel stole the scene. It must have been the day of the Harwich Smack Race. A wonderful fleet of smacks, bawleys and other assorted work boats and gaffers sailed its way past, heading downstream. Is there anything afloat, anywhere, that matches the perfect blend of form and function of the Essex smack?

There was old gaffer from Hong Kong.
He buy Essex smack for a song,
For Confucius he write: Greatest delight
Come to sailor whose bowsprit is long.

I slept on and off all day. The wind hauled to the southwest and blew up harder. A half gale was forecast. I was happy where I was. I could rest, observe life on this river, so different from our last sheltering spot at Plymouth, and think and perhaps write about the voyage we had made, while still afloat and sealed in our hermetic little world. At dusk I set my riding light, and, lulled into blissful oblivion by the chattering of a party of redshanks on the nearby shore, slept for ten hours.

23

Orwell River. Sunday, 9th July.

0800 Breakfast: meusli and milk. As I eat I observe the one blot on the otherwise soft and rural Suffolk landscape – the Felixstowe container wharves – just opposite and downstream from where I am anchored. The port is a marvel of engineering and efficiency. The nearest ship to me is the Greta Maersk *of Kobnhavn – Copenhagen to you and me. It is a puzzle how these container ships can carry so many containers on their decks without risk of capsize. I do some counting and calculation of containers on the* Greta Maersk's *deck. This suggests she could be carrying 1,938 containers on deck alone. At about 2,000 cubic feet per container, that is a heck of a volume. Further idle calculation. Result: the* Greta Maersk *of Kobnhavn could be carrying, on her deck alone, 77,200 wide screen televisions, or even 3.876 billion pairs of Y-fronts.*

1000 Today, a Sunday, the Orwell is a ghost river. The trickle of yachts seawards has become, still is, a trickle. Could it be that the good boaters of Suffolk prefer the warmth of a Sunday morning bed to the prospect of a near gale in the Wallet?

1400 Two o'clock on a July Sunday afternoon, at the mouth of the River Orwell – a river as well marina'd and yachted-out as any, and there are just three sails in sight... The thought occurs that if I had gone on to the Azores before turning back, an option I seriously considered, then I probably would have caught the full blast of the low that is causing the current blow. It came in, in full gale-bearing mode, via Sole and Plymouth yesterday, and has crossed north east to Malin. The barometer is the lowest we have seen it – 986 mb.

1700 As we get to low water and the wind eases somewhat and veers more to the west, I start thinking about the final leg home – about thirty nautical miles. It is strange indeed that this voyage, which started as a transatlantic blue water venture, is ending in the relative banality of a normal weekend sail.

1830 The wind, still 6/7, has gone to north-north-west. This is pretty much a leading wind for the Spitway, – the passage across the Gunfleet Sand into the Whitaker Channel that leads to Burnham. Never one to miss a fair wind I shall get my anchor and depart.

24

In a boisterous north-westerly, with just three panels set, we headed off down the coast, past the red headland of the Naze, past Walton Pier, out into a lively Wallet, with the tide under us. By eleven we were entering the Spitway, already halfway home on this final leg. The wind had eased little by little. We now had the full main set. As we turned to the south-west for the final run in to the Crouch the wind too pulled back further to the west and the tide turned against us.

We were just four or five miles from our holding position of two nights previously, but were now in a smooth sea with a ghosting breeze. We headed on, beating against the strengthening ebb. By two in the morning we had made a few more miles, but the breeze was dying. It seemed fitting to be once more becalmed, even this close to home. It seemed fitting that even this last stage of our journey should throw up yet another frustration to test us. Close to the Ridge buoy, in five metres of water, I threw the anchor overboard, to await the flood.

0500 The sun rises in a clear blue sky. The sea is smooth with the wind west 4. The last page of my log, and my last indelible pen is running out too. At 0600 I will get the anchor again and resume the beat into the Crouch, with the flood under us. The buoys

I can see from here – Ridge, Foulness, Swallowtail, Ron Pipe – are all old and familiar friends. Little Mingming will soon be home, after carrying me close to 2500 miles.

0600 I get the anchor – with difficulty. It is so well set that I have to sail it out. A lone golden plover flying north low over the water gilds this final morning.

0700 Working to windward in a light breeze and smooth sea.

0800 At the Buxey 1 and 2 cardinal markers we are passed by a Halcyon 27 – Vento Mara of Ipswich, reefed down in what is now a south west Force 3. It is a lovely quiet Monday morning, with all the old landmarks still in place.

At precisely 0901 hours, 28 seconds, we crossed the finishing line of the Mingming Challenge – a line between Holliwell Point to the north and Foulness Point to the south, marking the entrance to the River Crouch. I was of course the only participant, but I felt a quiet satisfaction. We had been at sea for just a few hours less than thirty-eight days. There had been no crises. We had encountered endless small adversities in the weather, but had never let them break our optimism.

Two hours later I picked up our Royal Corinthian Yacht Club mooring. The river was quiet, the clubhouse deserted. That suited me fine. We had slipped away quietly on a Good Friday morning, now we could return unnoticed. I put a few things in my little backpack and sat in the hatch, enjoying the peace, wondering if I really wanted to go ashore. Pete, one of the Rice and Cole yard men, passed in his work launch. I gave him a wave and held out my thumb, hitchhiker fashion. He pulled alongside and I jumped aboard. We pulled away from *Mingming*. I saw for the first time that she had acquired a beard of green along her waterline. She looked small, scruffy, faintly disreputable and, amongst the sleek Dragons, 707's, Squibs and Royal Corinthian One Designs that surrounded her, not worth a second glance. I couldn't resist a small smile. I knew otherwise.

Postscript

It was a few days before I was once again plugged in to the communications systems that now bind us so closely, and could construct a picture of what had happened to the other Jester Challengers. All the scenarios thrown up by my over-worked imagination proved to be laughably wide of the truth, except for one constant detail. First in to Newport, as always expected, had been Eric Andlauer in *Sterenn*, with a very creditable crossing time of thirty-one days. As well as *Mingming*, seven other Challengers had already retired. The severe weather that *Mingming* and I had, fortunately, only just brushed against had taken its toll on the rest of the fleet. Various gear failures – broken shrouds, leaks, electrical malfunctions, self-steering problems and so on – had forced boats back to land. There was nothing wrong with this. The Jester Challenge is about good seamanship and good judgement. If the majority of skippers decided that the prudent course of action was to retire gracefully, so be it. Despite the extremely challenging conditions for those taking the more northerly route, every yacht made port independently and in good order. That is how it should be.

Just one Challenger was still unaccounted for – Pete Hill in his Kingfisher 20 *Shanti* – whose tan junk sail was the last we had seen. A few days later the news came in. Pete had arrived in Newport, via the Azores route, in a time of forty-four days – a truly magnificent achievement.

Once again severe doubts about the decision to turn back began to plague me. Pete had had a perfect run, devoid of heavy weather, on the route I was proposing to take. On the other hand, he reported that hurricane conditions were expected off the US north-east coast just as he arrived in Newport. A few weeks earlier a British yacht had been lost in an early hurricane whilst en route from Newport to the Azores.

After a few days of torment I let it go. It didn't matter. To worry about what might have been is pointless beyond measure. *Mingming* had shown herself to be a little gem of a sea boat. There were a few small improvements to be made to bring her to the level of effortless manageability I was striving for. Back-of-the-envelope sketches for this and that were already accumulating. Two more Jester Challenges, one to the Azores, one to Newport, were scheduled for future years. I was already planning my next year's voyage, this time to the north. There was lots to do and not much time to do it in. Charts of remote seas and wind-swept coastlines were unwrapped from heavy parcels, then pored over, endlessly. My heart was singing. Nothing keeps the life-blood pulsing more strongly than the lure of new challenges, new dangers and fresh horizons.

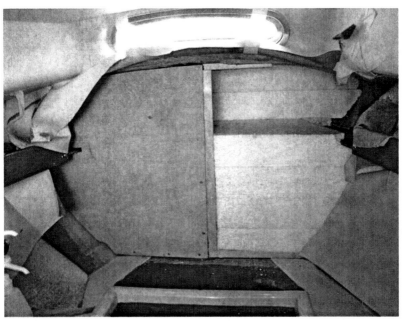

Making Mingming *unsinkable. Foam is packed solid behind a watertight bulkhead.*

Shipwright Darren Noonan replaces the washboards with solid mahogany.

The sliding hatch is replaced with a proper sealing hatch.

*The finished extra bridge deck and main hatch –
strong and seaworthy.*

Sailing trials on the River Crouch. Note the cockpit fill-in and sealed lazaret.

Mingming *alongside at Burnham-on-Crouch during winter trials.*

Drying out for a scrub-off at Osborne Bay, Isle of Wight.

Leaving Queen Anne Battery Marina under tow from Eric Andlauer and Sterenn *(photo: Frances Smart)*

Last farewell to the spectator boat
(photo: Frances Smart)

Running out into the Atlantic.

The chart table.

Below, looking aft.